THE CALM MIND CODE

Practical Psychology to Rebuild Your Peace Without Meditating for Hours or Deleting Your Personality

Harvey McGarry

Published by Authors Crib

www.AuthorsCrib.com

PREFACE

If you are reading this, I know something about you.

I know you are tired. Your brain is loud. It feels like you carry a tiny, screaming committee everywhere you go.

You've probably tried to fix it. Maybe you bought the crystals.

Maybe you tried to sit silently for an hour, only to discover that silence is where the monsters live.

This book is for the rest of us.

For the normal, slightly messed-up people who still want peace without having to fake spiritual enlightenment.

I promise this isn't fluff.

This is about practical tools.

It's about psychology that works in a noisy life.

We are going to stop trying to be perfect.

We are going to stop trying to control everything.

We are just going to learn how to turn the damn volume down.

Welcome to the code.

TABLE OF CONTENTS

CHAPTER ONE

The $9,000 Mistake: Why Your Brain Acts Like a Malfunctioning Smoke Alarm (and how this chronic noise costs you everything)

YOUR BRAIN IS LOUD.

Can you hear it right now?

That is the committee.

That little, screaming council that never adjourns.

It's the constant static. The low-frequency hum of worry that runs beneath every conscious thought.

You woke up with it. You drove to work with it. You are reading these words with it running in the background.

It doesn't just observe your life. It narrates it. It judges it. It constantly critiques your performance.

It keeps you trapped in a cycle of exhausting mental effort.

It tells you you're tired. It tells you you're inadequate. It tells you that success is possible only if you worry harder.

This noise is the problem.

It is the $9,000 mistake.

Not a specific $9,000 purchase. No. This is the cumulative, ongoing price tag for chronic mental chaos.

It's the cost of lost sleep. The energy wasted on arguments that only happened in your head. The opportunities you missed because the inner voice manufactured a terrifying risk assessment.

This noise is expensive. It costs you clarity. It costs you patience. It costs you connection.

Why do we listen to the worst voice in the room?

It's baffling, isn't it?

If you invited five people to your living room to discuss your future, and one of them started shouting apocalyptic nonsense, you would call security.

You would shut that person down.

Yet, when that voice lives inside your skull, we grant it absolute authority. We let it dictate our emotional state. We treat its screaming like sacred truth.

We need a better metaphor for what is happening up there.

It's not some grand spiritual deficiency. You aren't fundamentally broken.

Your hardware is just mis-calibrated.

Your brain is a smoke alarm. A very old, highly sensitive model.

Its only mission is survival. It scans the environment for threats. Fire. Predators. Social rejection.

When it detects something, anything—a shadow, a subtle change in routine, a memory—it screams. It activates the alarm protocol.

This worked flawlessly in the savannah. Your ancestors were grateful for that alarm.

It saved their lives from actual, physical fires.

But you don't live in the savannah anymore.

You live in a world of mortgages and emails and minor traffic jams.

The fire is gone. The physical threat is largely neutralized.

But the smoke alarm remains. And it is malfunctioning.

It is screaming because your boss used two periods instead of three in an instant message.

It is screaming because you remembered something embarrassing from 2012.

It is screaming about possible geopolitical crises you have zero control over.

It screams about the toast slightly burning in the kitchen.

This chronic noise is designed to keep you alert. It is succeeding wildly at that.

But it does not keep you safe. It just keeps you tired.

You are running on high alert. Always.

Your nervous system is constantly receiving high-volume input: DANGER! DANGER! FIX THIS!

But there is nothing to fix. Not right now.

We spend 80% of our mental resources reacting to things that have already happened or things that will likely never happen.

We are fighting ghosts with real energy.

Think about the energy required to simulate a full argument with your spouse, complete with tone, expressions, and counter-arguments. You feel the physical tension, right?

You are burning calories for an event that is 100% fabricated.

That is the tax of the malfunctioning smoke alarm.

We believe this noise is necessary. That is the core deception.

We confuse anxiety with diligence.

We think: If I worry about it hard enough, I will be prepared for anything.

Is that true?

Has your worrying ever truly solved a complex problem?

Or did the solution arise when you finally stopped worrying, took a deep breath, and thought clearly?

Worry is not thinking. Worry is rumination.

Worry is the cyclical, unproductive loop that offers the illusion of progress.

It feels like work. So we tolerate it. We even respect it.

We label ourselves as "deep thinkers" or "cautious planners."

But what are we cautious of? What are we really planning?

We are mostly planning for catastrophe. We are rehearsing failure.

And we are doing it exhaustingly.

The noise is unproductive.

Let's be blunt about this. Zero of the chronic anxiety loops you run daily actually contribute to your health, your wealth, or your relationships.

They actively subtract from all three.

They prevent you from seeing simple solutions. They cloud your judgment. They make you irritable.

The screaming committee doesn't provide valuable input. It just creates stress hormones.

And yet, we protect it. We feed it. We let it dominate our inner space.

The cost of this vigilance isn't just psychological.

It is intensely physical.

Living in a state of chronic high alert means your body never enters true rest and digest mode.

Your digestion suffers. Your sleep is fractured. Your immune system is constantly distracted by the phantom threats.

You feel scattered. You feel jittery. You feel permanently rushed, even when you have nowhere to go.

Why?

Because the alarm is still going off. BEEP! BEEP! The future might be bad! BEEP! BEEP! Remember that embarrassing thing you said!

Your body responds to this noise as if a bear were chasing you.

The adrenaline spike is real. The muscle tension is real.

But the source is fabricated. The threat is in the echo chamber of your own mind.

We need to stop conflating thinking with suffering.

You can think clearly without the volume at maximum setting.

In fact, you can only think clearly when the volume is turned down.

Right now, you are trying to navigate your life with a radio playing static at ear-splitting levels. You can barely hear the GPS instructions. You keep taking wrong turns. You keep crashing into minor obstacles.

Then you blame yourself for being a bad driver.

The problem isn't the driver. It's the environment. It's the noise.

Think about the sheer number of thoughts that pass through your mind in a day. Thousands. Tens of thousands.

How many of those are constructive?

How many are just re-runs of old scripts? How many are speculative fiction of upcoming disaster?

If you tracked the actual utility of your mental chatter, you would be horrified.

Most of it is junk. Most of it is waste. Most of it is the smoke alarm testing its battery every six minutes, just to be sure.

And here is the crucial mistake. The central flaw in the human operating system.

We personalize the noise.

When the alarm screams, we instantly merge with the scream.

The thought arises: I might lose my job.

And immediately, we become the person who is losing their job. We feel the shame. We feel the panic. We start writing the resignation speech in our heads.

The thought is an event. But we treat it as our identity.

We treat it as the absolute reality.

This is the key to escaping the $9,000 mistake.

You have to recognize that the noise is not you.

It is merely an occurrence in you.

It is a product of your evolutionary hardware running outdated software. It is a committee of panicked, well-meaning, but utterly destructive voices.

We have granted them too much power.

Imagine a busy city street.

Cars are honking. People are shouting. Sirens are wailing.

Your mind is that street. It's chaotic.

But you, the core self, are standing on the sidewalk, watching the chaos.

You are not the siren. You are not the honking car.

You are the observer. You are the listener.

But for years, you have stepped right into the street, grabbed the loudest siren, and yelled, "This is me!"

This confusion is why all traditional forms of "self-help" fail the normal, busy person.

They demand silence. They demand spiritual erasure. They tell you to empty the street.

That is unsustainable. The street will always be there. Life is noisy.

We are not going to try to achieve perfect silence.

We are going to do something much more practical.

We are going to learn how to operate the city street without stepping in front of the bus.

We are going to learn how to hear the sirens without merging with them.

We are going to find the volume knob.

The noise is exhausting. The noise is unproductive.

It is time to accept the diagnosis: You have a malfunctioning smoke alarm brain.

And it is costing you everything.

The first step toward peace is understanding exactly why that noise is so persistent. It's deeply programmed.

Let's uncover the evolutionary trap that keeps your brain obsessed with finding problems, even when everything is calm.

REVEALED: THE EVOLUTIONARY TRAP THAT MAKES YOUR BRAIN OBSESSED WITH FINDING PROBLEMS (AND THE 'BOREDOM TRIGGER' THAT GUARANTEES ANXIETY)

YOUR BRAIN EVOLVED IN THE JUNGLE.

It did not evolve for relaxation.

It was a tool for survival.

Its primary directive was simple: Scan for threats.

Find the problem. Fix the problem. Live another day.

This system worked perfectly.

We survived the woolly mammoths. We outsmarted the lions. We became the top of the food chain. But the scanner never received the memo.

The threat environment changed. We now live in safe homes. We have enough food. The true existential danger is largely gone.

But the brain is a process-driven machine. It demands data. It demands problems. It runs on anticipation.

It cannot just sit silently. It cannot be satisfied with neutrality. If you do not give it a challenge, it will create one.

This is the evolutionary trap.

The system is calibrated for high vigilance. When true threats disappear, that vigilance turns inward. It needs a subject. It needs a project.

It becomes obsessed with finding micro-problems.

It dissects an awkward email from three days ago. Problem identified. It forecasts financial ruin ten years from now. Problem identified. It reviews the worst conversation you ever had. Problem identified.

It is working. It is performing its function. It is solving problems that do not exist.

The Boredom Trigger

This is where true, modern anxiety starts. It is triggered by a lack of urgency.

When your life settles into a predictable routine, your brain perceives this as a flaw. Predictability feels like vulnerability.

A calm mind, to the primal brain, means you are letting your guard down. It sends up the alarm flare. It starts screaming warnings.

This manufactured noise is the boredom trigger.

The brain is saying: We are not busy enough. We are not anticipating enough danger. Speed up! Find the threat!

The feeling of anxiety is often nothing more than the energy of a powerful machine demanding input. It needs something to process.

If you give it silence, it panics. It views silence not as peace, but as suspicious blankness. It instantly starts filling that void with worst-case scenarios.

It is fundamentally a problem-solving computer running without any external problems. It refuses to shut down.

It starts working on the operating system itself. It finds flaws in your character. It finds flaws in your relationships. It generates crises where none existed ten minutes ago.

You are not anxious because you are weak. You are anxious because your survival mechanism is too good. It has been over-developed.

And it is profoundly, deeply bored.

It is running a simulation of catastrophe just to keep the lights on. This is the noise we must learn to manage. This is the truth of the evolutionary trap.

THE SECRET LINE: HOW TO SHIFT PRODUCTIVE PLANNING INTO DESTRUCTIVE RUMINATION IN 17 SECONDS FLAT

We need to talk about productive versus destructive.

Your brain loves to trick you here. It hides its most obsessive cycles under the friendly mask of "preparation" or "due diligence."

You start planning. You're being smart. You're being responsible. You're detailing the budget, or listing the steps for a complex project, or thinking about the upcoming talk with your boss. This is good. Planning is utility. It moves the ball forward.

But there is a trap.

The secret line is invisible. It's thin, like fishing wire. And crossing it takes less than 17 seconds.

Here is the difference, boiled down to the absolute core:

Productive planning seeks answers.

Destructive rumination seeks certainty.

Think about a tough conversation you need to have. Say, with a family member or a colleague.

Productive planning means you sit down and you list the facts. You write down the three key points you want to convey. You consider the single best outcome and the single worst outcome. You decide what your boundary is.

Then, crucially, you stop. You have a plan. You have utility.

Destructive rumination starts when you finish those steps, but instead of stopping, your brain hits the replay button.

You start inventing dialogue. You hear their voice getting defensive. You feel the heat in your chest. You pivot from focusing on the next action you can take to focusing on all the things you cannot control.

This is the shift. It's the 17-second pivot from utility to obsession.

The question you ask in planning is: What do I need to do now?

The question you ask in rumination is: What if I can't handle what happens later?

You are no longer solving a problem. You are narrating a disaster.

Let's look at a common, daily example: The big presentation next week.

Planning: You block out two hours on Tuesday to create the slide deck. You practice the introduction once. You review the data. You check the time slot. Done. You have maximized your influence over the outcome.

Rumination: You check the slide deck every ten minutes. You imagine forgetting your lines. You picture the CEO looking bored. You start researching alternative careers in case this presentation goes terribly wrong. You review every past presentation failure you have ever experienced.

Do you see the distinction?

The planning phase is finite. It requires effort, but it yields concrete steps.

The rumination phase is infinite. It requires exhaustion, but it yields nothing but anxiety.

You are running the same faulty script over and over again, not because you need new data, but because you are trying to force an emotional outcome: a feeling of safety.

You want the noisy brain to promise you that the future will be okay. And because the future can't make that promise, your brain keeps repeating the script, believing if it just worries hard enough, the certainty will appear.

It never does.

The secret line is crossed the moment the thought loop starts repeating without adding a single, actionable new step.

It's when you move from writing the presentation to mentally performing the funeral for your career. That shift is instant. We all do it.

Our job, moving forward, is to learn to recognize when we are no longer using the tool for production, but using it to generate pain. When you see that shift—when the answer becomes repetitive—the planning is over. It is time to put the tool down.

THE STOIC TRICK THAT INSTANTLY SEPARATES YOUR IDENTITY FROM THE NOISE (STOP BELIEVING THE SCREAMING COMMITTEE IS YOU)

THIS IS THE SINGLE MOST IMPORTANT DISTINCTION YOU WILL EVER make.

It is the core of all sanity.

You are not the voice in your head.

Let that sink in for a moment.

The constant, raging monologue is not you. It is merely an occurrence. It is a thing happening to you, or around you.

It is noise.

The greatest mistake normal, functional people make is believing the screaming committee is their identity. We merge with the thoughts. We fuse with the fear. We become the narrative.

I am worthless.

I will fail.

I am angry.

When you use the verb "to be" in connection with a judgment, you instantly lose the fight. You surrender your sovereignty.

You are the awareness that observes the chatter. You are the space in which the thoughts happen.

The Stoics mastered this separation centuries ago. They understood the mind produces thoughts the way the digestive system produces gas. It is a biological by-product of the machine. It is often necessary, sometimes helpful, and frequently foul.

But it is never you.

The trick is simple. It uses observation as a psychological crowbar.

You need to step back. You need to identify the separation between the "I" and the thought.

When a wave of panic hits, you stop the internal declaration: "I am panicking."

Instead, you adopt a neutral observer statement. This creates immediate, essential space.

I am noticing the sensation of panic.

I am having the thought that I am going to fail.

I recognize the feeling of defensiveness rising in my chest.

This linguistic shift changes everything. It reframes the event from a defining characteristic to a passing internal experience.

Imagine you are standing on the sidewalk. A train rushes past, loud and aggressive. You hear the noise. You feel the vibration. You acknowledge the train.

But you do not jump on the track. You do not suddenly decide you are the train.

Your internal monologue—your inner critic, your paranoid planner, your rehashing machine—is that train. It is roaring through your mind's station.

Your identity is the sidewalk. Solid. Unmoving. Observant.

This is the key. You are the observer. You are the consciousness that witnesses the noise.

Thoughts are events.

They pass. They arrive. They leave.

They require no response.

They demand no action.

You are not required to believe the train just because it is loud.

Practice this separation mercilessly. Every time you catch yourself defining yourself by a negative thought—"I am unproductive"—immediately pivot.

Say it out loud if you must.

"Ah, there is the thought, telling me I am unproductive."

Notice the difference. You have instantly stripped the thought of its authority. You have placed it outside the bounds of your core self.

This is not spiritual enlightenment. This is tactical psychological separation. It is the trick that prevents the noise from owning the room.

The screaming committee is not you. It is just your operating system running outdated, frantic software.

Your job is to update the software, not to become the glitch. Your identity is quiet. Your worth is fixed. It is the awareness that stays when the noise has faded.

Start acting like the silent, powerful observer you truly are. Let the train pass. Remain on the sidewalk.

WHY YOU ARE RUNNING ON EMPTY: THE PHYSICAL, EMOTIONAL, AND FINANCIAL TOLL OF CHRONIC HIGH ALERT

YOU FEEL HOLLOWED OUT.

Drained.

Like a laptop battery stuck permanently at three percent.

You are not lazy. You are not weak. You are merely exhausted by a war you cannot win. A war where the enemy is constantly broadcasting static from inside the wire.

Why are you running on empty?

Because you are living on chronic high alert. Your brain is convinced that disaster is imminent, every single moment. That malfunctioning smoke alarm is screaming about things that happened five years ago, or things that might happen next year, or things that aren't even real.

The body believes the alarm.

Your internal chemistry is flooded with the emergency response hormones: cortisol and adrenaline. Not for thirty seconds, but for thirty days. For three hundred days. Your system is constantly accelerating, anticipating the collision that never actually arrives.

This takes a physical toll. A heavy, aching, grinding toll.

Your sleep is shallow. You wake up tired because your brain spent the night rehearsing worst-case scenarios. Your muscles are tight. You carry tension in your neck and shoulders like two concrete weights. You are permanently braced for impact.

High alert destroys digestion. It suppresses your immune system. You get sick more easily. You get that creeping exhaustion that no amount of coffee can touch. This isn't stress. This is biological fatigue resulting from mismanaged internal dialogue.

Your thoughts are costing you your physical health.

The emotional price is equally devastating.

When you are fighting an invisible war inside your head, there is no bandwidth left for patience. For kindness. For joy.

You become brittle.

You snap at the people you love most because your reserve tank is dry. Every conversation feels like an invasion of your limited mental space. You start viewing your partner, your kids, or your colleagues as additional problems you must solve or manage, instead of sources of connection.

High alert erodes intimacy. It destroys trust.

If you are always expecting betrayal, disaster, or failure, that is the only reality you will be able to see. You are too busy trying to anticipate the relationship falling apart to actually enjoy the relationship standing up.

And yes, there is a financial toll.

Noise ruins focus. Chronic anxiety makes you a terrible strategic thinker. It forces you into short-term, impulsive decisions. You lose productivity at work because you spend 30% of your energy cycling through worry. You miss the big opportunities because your vision is clouded by small fears.

You buy quick fixes. The expensive vacation you can't enjoy. The retail therapy that lasts two hours. The supplements promising energy you are physiologically incapable of producing while the alarm is still blaring.

You are unconsciously trying to buy your way out of the high alert state.

We need to stop. We need to look at the mounting debt. The debt of sleepless nights. The debt of strained relationships. The debt of missed opportunities.

This is the true cost of listening to the screaming committee. You are running on empty because you have granted the noisiest, most destructive voice in the room unlimited energy consumption.

It's time to cut the power supply.

CHAPTER TWO

The Thought Defusion Code™: How to Hear the Voice Without Believing the Lie

OKAY. CHAPTER ONE WAS THE DIAGNOSIS.

We know your brain is a chaotic mess.

We know it's exhausting.

We know it costs you time, money, and sleep.

Now we get to the actual work.

This is the moment we stop analyzing the noise.

We start building the cage for it.

We are introducing The Thought Defusion Code™.

If you want the textbook definition, this is a core component of Acceptance and Commitment Therapy (ACT). But we aren't doing therapy here. We are doing mental maintenance. We are performing surgery on your operating system.

This is not meditation.

This is mental aikido.

It's a specialized skill developed for messy, normal people.

The goal isn't to stop the thoughts.

That's impossible.

Trying to stop a thought is like trying to stop the ocean with a tea strainer. You just get tired and wet.

The goal is simple: Stop believing the thoughts.

Stop treating mental noise like gospel truth.

The reason you are exhausted is because you are fused.

FUSION.

Think of fusion as instantaneous, total identification. When a scary or critical thought shows up, you don't hear a thought. You hear a fact. You hear a rule. You hear a prophecy of doom.

The thought is: "I am an imposter."

You feel: "I am an imposter."

The thought says: "You shouldn't have said that, you ruined everything."

You panic: "I have ruined everything."

The moment the thought arrives, your entire body and nervous system react as if the emergency is real. You merge with the language. You become the sentence.

You are treating the mental map as the actual territory.

This happens seventeen thousand times a day. We do it because we are language-based creatures. Our brains use words to survive. We learned early on that if the words say "Bear!" or "Fire!" you run. You don't pause and say, "I am noticing that I am having the thought that a bear is present."

That was useful when bears were common.

It is useless when the "bear" is a slightly awkward conversation you had three weeks ago.

The constant merging—the fusion—is what keeps you running on high alert. You cannot calm down if every sentence your brain spits out is treated like legally binding evidence of your inadequacy.

We need Defusion.

Defusion is the creation of psychological distance.

It is the act of stepping back far enough to realize:

Oh. That was just a sentence.

It was not a command.

It was not a law of physics.

It was a projection.

Defusion is simple linguistics applied to your internal life. You are changing the grammar of your existence. You are changing your relationship with language.

How do we do this?

It starts with acknowledging the distinction between the thought itself and the observer. The you who is listening.

The Stoics called this the ruling center. We call it The Observer. It's the calm, objective awareness that sits behind your eyes. It is the steady witness.

When you are fused, The Observer is asleep at the wheel. The screaming committee has taken over the PA system.

Our job is to wake The Observer up.

The simplest tool in the Defusion Code™ is the "I Notice" Technique.

Try this right now. Pick an intrusive thought that pops up often. Maybe it's "I'm not good enough." Maybe it's "I'm never going to finish this."

Don't fight it. Don't argue with it. Don't tell yourself to think positive things instead. That just fuses you to a different, equally exhausting fight.

Instead, wrap the thought in a phrase that describes the process of thinking.

If your brain screams, "I am going to screw up this presentation," you immediately shift your internal language.

Say: "I am noticing that I am having the thought that I am going to screw up this presentation."

Or even shorter: "I'm having a thought about screwing up."

Say it out loud if you can.

What happened?

The thought didn't disappear. That isn't the point.

But its grip loosened. Its authority vanished.

It went from being a direct command—an urgent fact—to being a recognized event. A piece of language that just floated across the screen of your awareness.

This is the power of distance.

Fusion is: Thought = Truth.

Defusion is: Thought = Language.

It sounds simple. But it is the difference between constant panic and stable action. When you defuse, you are reminding yourself, moment by moment, that you are not what your mind says you are.

Another essential technique in the Code is The Mental Voice Trick.

Your brain is incredibly serious. The inner critic uses the deep, serious, authoritative voice of a documentary narrator. It demands reverence. It commands belief.

We strip that authority away with absurdity.

The next time the inner critic screeches, "You are worthless and everyone hates you," do this:

Hear that thought in the voice of Elmo.

Or maybe a highly anxious chipmunk.

Or imagine it being sung dramatically in an opera voice.

This feels stupid, I know. But try it.

What happens? You laugh. Maybe just a tiny internal snort. That moment of laughter is radical defusion. It instantaneously breaks the serious, heavy authority the thought relies on.

Humor is a profound weapon against the noise. The committee hates to be laughed at. It cannot sustain its power when you treat its pronouncements like bad stand-up comedy.

We must also talk about the Sticky Thoughts.

Some thoughts feel heavy. They stick because they attach to core insecurities, or they promise to solve an important problem. They trick you into believing that if you just ruminate harder, you will find the solution.

They tell you: "You need to figure this out right now."

Fusion is wrestling with the thought until you are exhausted.

Defusion is treating the thought like an unsolicited sales call.

When a sticky thought arrives, you can use the Thank You technique.

Acknowledge the thought's presence, but reject its invitation to wrestle.

"Thanks, Brain, I appreciate the input. Not now."

"I see you, worry thought. I'll schedule you for later."

You don't fight the content. You interrupt the invitation.

Crucially, understand why most people fail at this. They believe that defusing a negative thought means they are dismissing a real problem.

"If I don't worry about my finances, I'll go broke!"

This is the central lie of the anxious brain. It has convinced you that worry is productive preparation.

It is not.

Worry is energy draining. Planning is energy directed.

Defusion allows you to separate the two.

If you defuse the thought, "I am definitely going to run out of money and live in a box," you create the space to ask a much better question:

"What is one productive action step I can take right now regarding my finances?"

See the difference? Fusion keeps you paralyzed by fear. Defusion frees your energy to act on your values, even while the fear thought is still present.

This is the key distinction of The Code. You don't wait for the noise to stop to start living. You live with the noise.

Think of your thoughts as passengers on a bus.

The bus is your life. You are the driver.

Fusion is letting the screaming passengers (The Critic, The Paranoid Planner) take the steering wheel. They decide where the bus goes. And they drive terribly, often into ditches.

Defusion is realizing you are the driver. The passengers are still there. They are still loud. They are still yelling suggestions, insults, and dire warnings. But their yelling is just noise in the cabin.

You hear them. You acknowledge them.

But you keep your hands firmly on the wheel. You drive the bus where you want it to go. Towards your values.

The ultimate goal of the Thought Defusion Code™ is not to silence the committee. It is to strip the committee of its voting power.

It's about recognizing that thoughts are simply language. They are descriptions. They are opinions. They are the brain's best, but often worst, guess at reality. They are not the truth.

They are not who you are.

You hear the lie. You acknowledge the lie. You look the lie directly in the face. Then you move your feet toward what matters anyway.

We are just changing three small words in your internal dictionary:

Instead of "I am angry," you say, "I am having the feeling of anger."

Instead of "I failed," you say, "I am having the thought that I failed."

It seems small. But this small linguistic shift is what allows The Observer to sit up, stretch, and reclaim the driver's seat.

Practice this code constantly. Not just when the big thoughts hit, but when the small ones do, too.

"I need coffee immediately."

"I am noticing that I am having a strong desire for caffeine."

"That person looked at me weird."

"I am noticing the thought that I am being judged."

Build this muscle of separation. Make defusion your default setting.

The voice is still there. But now it's just background static. It's a distant radio playing a song you don't like. You don't have to listen to the lyrics. You don't have to change the station. You just turn your attention back to the road.

You decide who drives. Not the noise.

THE INVISIBLE FORCE FIELD: 3 NON-MEDITATIVE WAYS TO CREATE SPACE BETWEEN YOU AND YOUR SCARIEST THOUGHTS

You do not need to sit on a cushion.

You do not need to chant anything.

When I talk about creating space, people immediately think of meditation. They think of forced silence. They think of painful mindfulness exercises where the point is to empty the mind.

No. We are not emptying the mind.

That's like trying to stop the ocean from having waves. It's futile.

We are just building an invisible force field. We are learning how to hear the thought without automatically granting it authority. We are creating a subtle, immediate distance between you and the psychological event that is occurring inside you.

This is less about spirituality and more about cognitive engineering. It's the highest leverage move you can make against anxiety.

Here are three practical, non-meditative ways to build that force field, right now, in the middle of a traffic jam or a boring meeting.

1. THE 'I NOTICE' PREFIX

THIS IS SIMPLE. THIS IS POWERFUL. THIS IS THE FIRST STOP FOR defusion.

When a stressful, scary, or self-critical thought pops up, your brain merges with it instantly.

The thought: I am going to mess this up.

The merger: You become a person who is messing up. You feel the shame immediately.

To create the force field, you add a simple prefix to the thought.

You state, silently or aloud:

I am having the thought that I am going to mess this up.

I am having the thought that everyone secretly hates me.

I am noticing the physical sensation of dread.

See the difference?

When you say, "I am having the thought," you turn the thought from an active reality into an object you are observing. It is no longer you that is failing; it is your brain that is generating a specific piece of data.

You become the person watching the committee instead of being forced to chair the meeting.

This takes less than a second. It requires no closed eyes. It is pure distance. It shifts you from the content of the thought to the process of thinking.

You are not the thought. You are the one noticing the thought. Practice this when the stakes are low—the moment you think, I forgot the milk, immediately add the prefix: I am noticing the thought that I forgot the milk. Build the muscle when it's easy, so it's strong when the real monsters arrive.

2. THE MENTAL RADIO STATION HACK

YOUR INNER VOICE IS RELENTLESS. IT ACTS LIKE A BROKEN RADIO station that only plays static, doom, and retrospective shame.

When a deeply frightening thought—maybe about a future health issue or a past relational mistake—starts dominating, treat it like noise pollution.

You don't need to fight it. You don't need to change the channel. You just need to adjust the volume.

Imagine your thoughts are being broadcast from a speaker right next to your ear. That's fusion. That's high volume.

To create space, you simply decide to move the speaker.

A scary thought arrives. Instead of engaging with the content (e.g., arguing back, trying to solve the hypothetical crisis), you externalize it.

Visualize the thought streaming from an old radio on the top shelf of the room. The voice is still talking, but now it's distant. It's slightly fuzzy.

Maybe you imagine the thought on a tiny black and white television screen 20 feet away. You can see the text—the warning, the criticism—but it's not consuming your entire field of vision.

The key here is non-engagement. You don't grab the radio and smash it. You don't try to shout over the TV. You just acknowledge that it's playing in the background while you continue doing what you need to do (like driving, working, or making coffee).

This trains you in selective attention. The thought is present. But you are choosing to allocate 5% of your processing power to the sound, instead of 100%.

3. THE CARTOON VOICE DEFLATOR

WHAT GIVES A NEGATIVE THOUGHT ITS POWER?

Seriousness.

Anxiety and self-criticism thrive on gravity. They demand that you treat them as life-or-death warnings, even when they are about trivial things.

If you can instantly deflate the seriousness of the thought, you cripple its power to command your behaviour.

This is the fastest, funniest hack for defusion, and it works because it leverages the part of your brain that knows how to differentiate reality from absurdity.

The brain screams: You are completely unprepared for that presentation. You will be exposed as a fraud.

In that split second, hear that thought delivered in the voice of someone utterly ridiculous.

Try it in the voice of Elmo. Try it in the voice of a deep-sea diver underwater. Try it sung like an opera singer lamenting a lost puppy.

Or, my personal favourite: deliver the criticism in the booming, exaggerated voice of a 1940s movie trailer announcer.

"In a world where one man forgot to hit 'send' on the email... his life will never be the same! Coming soon to a theatre near you, the ultimate failure!"

When you do this, you cannot remain merged with the thought. The seriousness instantly collapses into a giggle.

Laughter is the ultimate cognitive defusion tool. It proves to your nervous system that the threat is, in fact, not a threat at all. It is a psychological drama that you just cast with entirely inappropriate actors.

These three methods—the prefix, the radio station, and the cartoon voice—are your invisible force field. They require zero silence and zero deep breathing. They are mental edits you perform mid-sentence.

Start using them today. You will be amazed how quickly the committee quiets down when you stop letting them sit at the head of the table.

SHOCKING: MOST INTRUSIVE THOUGHTS ARE FUELLED BY MISIDENTIFIED EMOTIONS (THE DIAGNOSTIC CHECK THAT SHUTS THEM DOWN)

We believe our intrusive thoughts are problems we need to solve.

We treat them like highly detailed threats.

We analyse the content. We argue with the logic. We try to prove them wrong.

This is the central mistake.

The vast majority of truly disruptive, repeating, intrusive thoughts are not fuelled by logic. They are fuelled by misidentified emotions.

They are symptoms, not the disease.

Consider the feeling of generalized, low-grade discomfort. Maybe it's a tight chest. Maybe it's a buzz in your hands. Maybe it's just a persistent, irritating restlessness.

We are terrible at identifying what this feeling actually is.

Is it frustration? Is it shame? Is it low-level grief?

If you don't give that internal energy a precise, honest name, your brain panics.

Your brain is a storytelling machine. It hates ambiguity more than anything else. It sees that uncomfortable emotional energy sitting there, unnamed, and assumes there must be a catastrophe to explain it.

It generates a narrative to match the intensity of the feeling.

It says, "Why am I feeling this way? I must be feeling this way because I messed up my relationship. I must be feeling this way because I'm definitely going to fail the next five years."

That narrative becomes the intrusive thought.

The thought is not the root cause. The thought is just the brain's clumsy attempt to translate a raw emotional signal into a recognizable story.

The discomfort came first. The story came second.

The shock here is that you spend all your energy battling the story, which is just smoke. You never tackle the fire, which is the unnamed emotion.

So, how do you shut it down? You perform a diagnostic check.

You must stop asking, "What does this thought mean?"

You must start asking, "What emotion is fuelling this noise?"

The next time a horrible thought—a rehearsal of shame, a prediction of doom, a wave of self-criticism—washes over you, pause.

Do not engage the content.

Ask yourself these four precise questions instead:

1. If I strip away the words and the narrative, what is the raw feeling? (Is it anger? Is it sadness? Is it disappointment?)

2. Where is this emotion sitting in my body right now? (Is it a heavy feeling in my gut? Is it tension in my jaw?)

3. How old does this emotion feel? (Does this shame feel like adult failure, or does it feel like a nine-year-old being yelled at?)

4. Is the thought I am having right now truly a warning about a future event, or is it merely an explanation my brain created for the anxiety I already feel?

Most often, the intrusive thought is simply the explanation.

When you realize that the paralyzing fear about your career is actually a translation of the deep exhaustion you feel from working sixty hours a week, the thought loses its power.

The brain thought the exhaustion meant failure. The thought said, "Quit now before they realize you're incapable."

But the feeling was just the deep, bodily need for rest.

You don't need to solve the crisis narrative. You need to name the emotional reality.

Once you name the true emotion—exhaustion, grief, simple boredom—the energy fuelling the intrusive story often dissipates immediately. The brain says, "Oh. Okay. It's just tiredness. Not the end of the world."

The Diagnostic Check forces you to separate the raw feeling from the intellectual interpretation.

You stop trying to fight the narrative in your head and start honouring the feeling in your body.

When you refuse to engage the smoke and instead address the fire, the alarm finally starts to quiet down.

THE PARADOX OF PEACE: WHY INACTION IS THE MOST POWERFUL ACTION WHEN THE BRAIN DEMANDS A SOLUTION

This is the toughest psychological pivot you will ever attempt.

Your brain is a machine built for completion.

It despises open loops.

It sees an anxious thought—

A potential disaster.

A theoretical insult.

A future embarrassment.

The brain immediately flags it as critical data.

It demands a reaction.

It demands a solution.

It demands a final, perfect resolution to the hypothetical problem it just created.

This is where we always fail.

We are trained that action equals power.

We are taught that ignoring a problem is weakness.

This is true in the real world.

But the mental world operates by opposite rules.

The thought is not a real problem.

It is only a prompt.

It is bait.

When you engage the thought, you validate its existence.

When you try to solve the anxiety, you confirm the danger is real.

You feed the loop.

The paradox of peace is this: Sometimes, the only winning move is not to play.

When the mental chatter arrives—loud, urgent, insisting you must rehearse that argument or finalize that worst-case scenario—your most powerful response is silence.

It is stillness.

It is refusal.

We call this strategic inaction.

It feels horrible at first.

It feels like negligence.

It feels like leaving the alarm blaring.

Your internal Fixer screams, "But we must do something!"

The action you need to take is the radical choice to do nothing at all to the thought itself.

You acknowledge the thought.

"There is the worry about money."

"There is the memory of that stupid thing I said."

You observe it. You name it.

Then you stop.

You do not analyse it.

You do not chase it down the dark alley of "What if?"

You do not try to debate the voice.

Debate is engagement. Engagement is fuel.

When you refuse to take the bait, the thought has nowhere to go.

It is an engine without gas.

A thought cannot sustain itself without your active participation.

It needs you to give it gravity.

It needs you to write the next sentence in its story.

When the brain screams, "I need a solution now!" you respond by breathing.

You respond by dropping the internal rope.

You respond by waiting.

It is hard. It is unnatural.

But every single time you choose inaction over analysis, you teach your brain a profound lesson:

This thought is not compulsory.

This feeling is temporary.

This hypothetical does not require my energy.

Inaction starves the thought.

Inaction dissolves the problem.

Inaction is the highest form of power in the war against mental noise.

It is the ultimate cognitive defusion move.

ARE YOU STUCK IN THE TERRITORY? HOW BELIEVING YOUR MENTAL MAP DESTROYS PEACE IN 7 KEY AREAS OF YOUR LIFE

YOU HAVE A MAP IN YOUR HEAD.

Everyone does.

It is your mental representation of the world. It includes your beliefs about who you are. The stories you tell yourself about how the world works. Your projections about tomorrow.

This mental map is incredibly useful. It helps you decide which street to take. It helps you remember that fire is hot.

But what happens when you confuse the map with the actual territory?

Disaster.

You wouldn't try to drink the picture of water on a menu. You wouldn't try to eat a map of a sandwich. Those things are representations. They are symbols. They are not the real thing.

Yet, we spend 80% of our waking lives attempting to eat the map.

This is cognitive fusion.

It is the technical term for stopping the separation. It's when you believe the voice in your head is telling you the literal, unvarnished, immediate truth.

When you are fused, the thought is the fact. The story is the reality. The judgment becomes your identity.

It destroys peace because the map is inherently flawed. It is often old, messy, and designed by fear. When you are fused, you don't realize you are fighting paper dragons. You think you are fighting reality.

Here is how believing the map instead of living in the territory demolishes your peace in key areas of your life.

1. CAREER AND CONFIDENCE

The Map: "I am an imposter. They are going to find out I don't belong here."

When you fuse with this thought, you stop preparing for the meeting. You start preparing for the inevitable exposure. You withdraw. You minimize your good work. You make decisions based on anticipating failure, which then makes failure more likely. You are reacting to a mental prediction, not to the demands of the actual job. Peace is destroyed because you never allow yourself to settle into your competence.

2. RELATIONSHIPS AND INTIMACY

The Map: "They are upset with me. I know it. They are pulling away."

You haven't checked the facts. You haven't asked. You just decided based on a slight change in tone or a delayed text. Because you are fused with the anxiety of the map, you start acting defensive or cold. You punish the other person for a crime they only committed in your head. You create conflict based entirely on an assumption. The territory—the actual relationship—never stood a chance against your internal narrative.

3. SELF-WORTH AND IDENTITY

The Map: "I am permanently flawed. I am not worthy of good things."

Fusion turns a judgment into an essential feature of your personality. It is not something you are thinking. It is something you are. This belief guides every choice. You avoid promotions. You settle in relationships. You deny yourself joy because the map dictates your worthiness is zero. You don't try to fight the thought. You try to accommodate the flaw.

4. DECISION PARALYSIS

The Map: "If I choose Path A, the worst possible outcome will happen. If I choose Path B, I will regret it forever."

The fused brain turns future possibilities into concrete memories of failure. It creates a certainty of doom that doesn't exist. You don't feel like you are choosing between two options. You feel like you are choosing between two guaranteed disasters. You stay stuck. You freeze. Inaction feels safer than the certainty of mental catastrophe.

5. HEALTH AND BODY IMAGE

The Map: "My body is wrong. I am disgusting. I will never be able to change."

This is the ultimate trap of negative self-labelling. When you are fused, the words are the truth. You don't see a body that needs movement or fuelling. You see a permanent problem. This shuts down motivation. Why exercise if the label is permanent? You stop taking effective action because the internal map has already declared the war over.

6. RECURRENCE OF PAST SHAME

The Map: "Remember that thing you did in 2018? You should feel the burning shame right now."

The brain has the ability to make a past event feel instantly present. Fusion means you let it. You allow an incident that is over—gone, ended—to colonize your present emotional state. You are trapped living in the emotional landscape of yesterday, rehearsing lines and arguments that died years ago. You are not experiencing the territory of this moment.

7. FORECASTING DOOM (GENERAL ANXIETY)

The Map: "The worst possible scenario is about to happen. Prepare for impact."

This is the central function of the anxious map. It constantly projects catastrophe. When you are fused, you begin reacting to this forecast with the same physiological intensity you would use to react to a physical threat. Your cortisol spikes. Your breathing shallows. You are emotionally exhausted, yet nothing threatening is actually happening. You are living the future collapse right now.

Cognitive defusion, the core skill we are developing, is learning to see that paper map for what it is. It is not the territory.

It is just a representation.

It is not a command. It is not a fact. It is only a thought.

When you can hear the thought, acknowledge the map, but choose to live in the territory, the noise loses its power instantly.

CHAPTER THREE

BREAKOUT: Escaping the Overthinker's Treadmill That Wastes 19 Hours of Your Week

YOU ARE EXHAUSTED.

You have to admit it.

Not body tired. But brain fried.

This is the cost of the Overthinker's Treadmill.

It's the most subtle, destructive lie your brain tells you. It makes you feel productive. It makes you feel responsible. It tells you that by analyzing the problem from 17 different angles, you are somehow preventing disaster.

You are not.

You are spinning in place.

This machine, this mental looping, is the most profound waste of human energy imaginable. It simulates work. It demands full emotional attention. It delivers zero results.

It's high effort, zero progress.

We estimated 19 hours a week. Think about that. That is nineteen hours—a full workday plus three additional evenings—spent replaying arguments, forecasting doom, or meticulously planning for scenarios that have a 3% chance of occurring.

Nineteen hours of your finite life. Burned.

We are going to stop respecting the loop.

We are going to learn how to hit the emergency stop button.

The fundamental shift needed for this chapter is recognizing that rumination is not processing. It is recycling.

When you process something—a trauma, a decision, a relationship—you move through it. You gain clarity. You reach a conclusion. That conclusion might be painful, but it is a conclusion. It has momentum.

Rumination is stalling.

It is running the same outdated software again and again, waiting for a different error message. It's the brain stuck in an internal argument where both sides are you, and neither side has access to new information.

The noise is not movement.

The noise is paralysis dressed in activity.

The reason these loops feel so compelling is that they touch on core areas of perceived threat: reputation, safety, love, or competence. Our brain's job is to protect these things. When it identifies a threat, it demands immediate, thorough analysis.

But the machine is poorly calibrated.

It doesn't know the difference between a charging tiger and a slightly rude email from a colleague. Both trigger the high-alert analysis cycle. Both lock you onto the treadmill.

We must learn the difference between Productive Thinking and the Loop.

Productive thinking has utility. It results in a non-thought action.

Example: I need to solve this budget shortfall.

Action: I will create a spreadsheet. I will contact the accounting department. I will dedicate 30 minutes to brainstorming solutions.

That's movement. That's utility.

The Loop has no utility. It results in more thoughts.

Example: I can't believe I might have a budget shortfall. Why am I always struggling? What will people think of me? I should have taken that other job five years ago. This is going to ruin everything. I feel sick.

That is the treadmill. Notice the switch. It moved from a solvable problem (the shortfall) to a cosmic judgment (why am I always struggling?). It moved from the present to five years ago. It moved from action to pure emotional forecasting.

Your first step off the treadmill is radical honesty.

You must catch the exact moment the switch flips.

You are not planning. You are worrying.

You are not preparing. You are rehearsing shame.

You are not calculating risk. You are manufacturing fear.

This is where the power of Defusion (Chapter 2) comes back into play, but amplified. We are not just observing the thought; we are interrupting the pattern.

The problem is the cyclical nature itself. The pattern feeds the emotion, and the emotion fuels the pattern. It is self-sustaining energy—a dark little generator running exclusively on your stress.

We break this generator by imposing structure where the loop demands chaos.

How do you interrupt a spiral that feels all-consuming?

You use the structure. You use the code.

The most potent tool against rumination is the scheduled limitation.

Your brain thinks if it stops worrying now, disaster will strike immediately. It believes it is protecting you by staying alert. We need to respect that instinct, but domesticate it.

You introduce the concept of "Worry Time."

This might sound absurdly simple, but it is one of the most effective psychological interventions available for chronic worry.

You designate a specific 15-minute window every day. Let's say 4:45 PM.

That is your Worry Zone.

When a loop starts—I need to figure out how to pay that bill, I need to know if they are mad at me, I need to know if I said the right thing last Tuesday—you acknowledge the thought immediately.

You label it: Rumination. Loop detected.

Then you gently, firmly redirect it: "Thank you for the input. This issue is scheduled for 4:45 PM today."

You do not argue with it. You do not try to solve it. You just defer it.

Why does this work?

It satisfies the brain's need for recognition. It says, "Yes, this is important, and we will address it."

But it breaks the immediate, uncontrolled demand for attention. You take back the authority over when the thought is processed.

When 4:45 PM arrives, you sit down. You open a notebook. You dedicate 15 minutes to writing down every fear, every worry, every future forecast. No filtering. Just output.

Then, the moment the 15 minutes are up, you stop.

You physically close the notebook. You stand up. You move your body. You do not return to that list until the next scheduled time.

Often, by 4:45 PM, the thoughts that seemed catastrophic at 11:00 AM have lost their potency. The brain realizes the crisis didn't materialize just because you deferred the worry.

You teach your system that deferral is safe.

This is pure, practical stoicism in action: You are controlling your attention, which is the only thing you truly own.

But what about the deep, immediate spirals? The moments where the worry is a full-body experience?

You need a hard stop.

This is where Vague Mindfulness fails you. Telling a spiraling person to "just breathe" is often useless. They need concrete, non-negotiable tactics that interrupt the chemistry, not just the philosophy.

We are implementing the Hard Pivot.

When you feel the emotional surge—the pit in your stomach, the heat in your face, the racing thoughts—you must immediately pivot from analysis to sensor input.

Your brain is in the Territory of the Past or the Territory of the Future. We are bringing it back to the map of Right Now.

The Hard Pivot uses a simple three-step process designed to shift your attention from abstract concepts (shame, money, failure) to concrete reality (light, texture, temperature).

STEP ONE: FIND THREE COLORS

Immediately look around the room. Not generally. Specifically. Name three distinct colors you see. The exact shade of the wall. The specific blue of the pen. The dirty white of the ceiling tile.

Say them out loud if you can, or whisper them. This forces your higher brain function to stop running the loop and engage the visual processing centre in a new, low-stakes task.

STEP TWO: ENGAGE THREE TEXTURES

Touch something. The fabric of your shirt. The smooth wood of the desk. The cold ceramic of the coffee cup. Really feel it. Concentrate on the sensation. Is it rough? Is it cool? Is it slightly sticky?

This grounds you in the immediate physical world. It shuts down the theoretical chatter. The brain cannot efficiently run the past-future loop while concentrating deeply on sensory input.

STEP THREE: NAME ONE ACTION

THIS IS THE MOST CRITICAL COMPONENT. IT FORCES THE TRANSITION from analysis (the treadmill) to utility (the breakout).

Ask yourself one stoic question:

"What is the single, non-thought action I can take right this second that moves me forward 1%?"

It must be tangible. It must be immediate.

If you are worrying about debt, the action might be: "I will open the bank app." Not "I will solve all my debt." Just the 1% move.

If you are spiralling about a relationship argument, the action might be: "I will write down the single thing I want to communicate, without editing."

If the loop is about a mistake you made five years ago, the action is: "I will close my eyes and let the memory be there, but I will consciously flex and relax my toes ten times." (A physical act to override the mental loop.)

The beauty of the Hard Pivot is its simplicity and its reliance on sensory data. It is a neurological override.

It is impossible to be fully absorbed in the abstract panic of the future while consciously counting the blue items on your desk. You cannot do both simultaneously.

You choose the reality of the present.

The Overthinker's Treadmill thrives on the illusion of urgency. It demands that everything be fixed right now.

The counter-strategy is purposeful slowness and specific structure.

The moment you recognize the loop, you gain power.

You don't need to banish the voice. You don't need to achieve some perfect, silent state.

You just need to interrupt the energy flow.

The loop requires your time and your belief that it is important. When you interrupt it, when you label it as mere recycling, you withdraw your belief.

That is the breakout.

It is accepting that 90% of your current stress is self-generated. It is not externally required. It is a habit. And habits can be broken by consistent, targeted interference.

Get off the treadmill. Your actual life is waiting right beside it. Take the single step forward. The real world is quieter than your head. Trust me on that.

THE 'WORRY SIGNATURE': A SIMPLE INVENTORY TO CATEGORIZE YOUR MOST DESTRUCTIVE MENTAL LOOPS (FORECASTING DOOM VS. REHEARSING SHAME)

WE NEED TO STOP TREATING WORRY LIKE A SINGLE LARGE CLOUD.

It's not.

Worry is specific. It has patterns. It has a rhythm unique to you.

Think of it like a repeating vinyl record. You keep dropping the needle in the same groove. The goal isn't to destroy the record player. It's just to recognize which song is playing.

This recognition is crucial. When you can name the loop, you gain distance from it. It stops being you. It becomes something you are doing.

We call this your Worry Signature.

Grab a mental checklist. Which one of these consumes the most headspace? You might run all three, but usually, one is the tyrant that dominates your mental landscape.

FORECASTING DOOM: THE PRE-EMPTIVE DESTROYER

THIS IS THE ANXIETY OF THE FUTURE.

It's the "What if?" loop.

It screams about things that haven't happened yet.

Your brain assumes its job is to anticipate every possible disaster. It believes if you worry hard enough, you can somehow stop the train wreck from occurring.

This loop is characterized by high-stakes visualization.

You mentally rehearse the failure of the presentation. You run the scenario where the relationship collapses. You imagine the moment you run out of money, five years before it's even plausible.

It's a perpetual state of planning for disaster that consumes all energy available for productive action today.

The feeling signature: Dread, tension in the gut, a hyper-alertness that masquerades as preparation.

Ask yourself: Am I actively solving a problem, or am I creating a tragedy I cannot yet prevent?

REHEARSING SHAME: THE RELENTLESS REWIND

THIS IS THE ANXIETY OF THE PAST.

It's the "I should have said..." loop.

This signature locks you in the archives of previous mistakes, embarrassments, and perceived failures.

It doesn't seek insight; it seeks punishment.

The committee in your head forces you to relive the cringe-worthy moment from high school. Or that stupid thing you said at the meeting last week. You spend twenty minutes in the shower formulating the perfect apology to a person who has already forgotten the incident.

This is where you try to verbally destroy yourself over things that cannot be changed. You keep pressing rewind, hoping this time the scene will play out differently. It never does.

This loop is destructive because it attaches your current identity to an obsolete moment. It tells you, "You are the sum total of your worst decision."

The feeling signature: A deep, heavy regret, the urge to hide, acute self-criticism.

Ask yourself: Am I analysing this event for a future lesson, or am I simply inflicting pain on myself for something that is over?

REHEARSING ARGUMENTS: THE INTERNAL DÉFENSE ATTORNEY

THIS IS THE ANXIETY OF VALIDATION AND RELATIONAL CONTROL.

This loop is focused on proving your worth, justifying your actions, or winning an argument that exists only in your skull.

You might spend forty minutes walking the dog, detailing the perfect counter-argument for a co-worker you haven't spoken to yet.

You prepare the evidence. You practice the tone of voice. You craft the email that proves your innocence, the one you will never send.

This signature is driven by the fear of being seen as wrong, weak, or misunderstood. You seek certainty through verbal mastery, even when the other person isn't present, or doesn't care.

It drains your ability to be present because you are always preparing for battle. You are fighting ghost enemies.

The feeling signature: Agitation, a racing pulse, subtle resentment, and profound distraction.

Ask yourself: Is this mental energy leading to connection, or is it building walls of justification?

Look at these three categories. Which one is the loudest? Which loop do you fall into when you are tired, bored, or stressed? That is your dominant Worry Signature.

You are not broken if you run all three. You are human.

But understanding your signature is the moment we start the interruption. We stop giving the general name "worry" to highly specific, interruptible habits.

The moment you realize, "Ah, I'm not just worried, I'm engaging in an aggressive episode of Rehearsing Shame again," the power shifts.

You now have a name for the beast.

And the named beast is always easier to defuse.

THE WORRY TAX: CALCULATING THE EXACT ENERGY AND TIME DEBT WORRY COSTS YOU (HINT: IT'S NEVER PRODUCTIVE)

You think worry is productive.

You call it mental planning.

You call it foresight.

You believe that if you stress hard enough, you can solve the future.

This is the single biggest operational error your brain makes.

It is the lie that keeps you trapped.

Worry is not preparation.

Worry is debt.

It is the most expensive, high-interest tax you pay every single day.

And you pay it on a potential problem that probably won't even happen.

Let's calculate the cost.

First, the energy debt.

This is the physical tax.

You burn real fuel.

You are running on cortisol.

Your nervous system is constantly on red alert.

That tension in your neck? That's the worry tax.

The constant churn in your stomach? Tax.

The sleepless nights spent designing escape routes for scenarios that exist only in your mind? Tax.

It is a metabolic waste.

You are exhausting your body fighting a phantom enemy.

Your energy reserves are spent before you even face a real challenge.

You start the day depleted.

You start the week on empty.

Because you paid the Worry Tax on Sunday night.

Second, the time debt.

This is the ultimate, non-refundable cost.

Where did the last hour go?

You spent twenty minutes rehearsing a difficult conversation.

You spent fifteen minutes reliving a mistake from high school.

You spent the rest of the time forecasting three potential doom scenarios for next month's budget meeting.

That time is gone.

Irretrievably lost.

Did those forty minutes produce a single, executable action item?

No.

Did they change the outcome of the past?

No.

Did they make the future less likely?

No.

You simply experienced the stress of the event three times without actually solving anything.

That is the definition of unproductive labour.

Worry feels like working. It occupies the brain. It demands intense focus. It generates noise.

But it is pure mental static.

It offers zero ROI.

Zero return on investment.

It is an expenditure with no gain.

Productive planning identifies a variable, determines the best two courses of action, and sets a date to execute. That's it. It's done. It's stored.

Rumination identifies a variable, explores 7,000 impossible outcomes, loops the fear, generates physiological stress, and leaves the variable unsolved.

You must stop confusing the feeling of frantic mental activity with actual utility.

You think: I must be worried, or I won't be careful.

Wrong.

You can be careful while remaining calm.

You can be prepared without being depleted.

In fact, the calmer you are, the better your preparation will be.

Worry is just noise that dulls your cognitive edges.

It steals the sharp focus you need for real solutions.

It guarantees you will be tired when the real challenge finally arrives.

The debt is too high.

Stop paying the tax.

Stop allowing your valuable time and finite energy to be spent on fictional problems.

You are running a debt economy in your mind.

It's time to declare mental bankruptcy on worry.

——★–★–★——

HOW TO GROUND YOURSELF IN 4 SECONDS FLAT: PRACTICAL, SECULAR TACTICS THAT REJECT VAGUE 'MINDFULNESS' ADVICE

Your brain hates the present moment.

It views 'now' as empty space.

A vacuum that must be filled with future planning or past reviewing.

When that malfunctioning smoke alarm starts shrieking, the last thing you need is some gentle advice about observing the clouds. We are rejecting that fluff. We are rejecting the slow, vague, "just breathe" advice that makes you feel incompetent when you can't achieve inner peace while actively having a panic attack.

You need a tactical stop sign.

A hard reset for your internal operating system.

These are secular, physical hacks. They are designed to drag your mind out of the abstract (worry, dread, what-if) and lock it into the concrete (gravity, texture, temperature).

Here is how you ground yourself in 4 seconds flat.

The goal is interruption, not meditation.

TACTIC 1: THE SENSORY DATA DUMP

THE PROBLEM WITH AN OVERTHINKING BRAIN IS THAT IT'S SOLVING an abstract problem. It's debating imaginary situations. The way to stop it is to give it a mandatory, immediate, physical task.

Your inner critic is a brilliant liar, but it is terrible at data entry.

The moment you feel the spiral begin—the tightness, the racing pulse, the future catastrophizing—you do this. You pivot your focus to mandatory physical data collection.

Find five things you can see, right now.

Do not think about them. Do not judge them. Just name them.

The dust on the bookshelf. The seam of the shirt cuff. The exact shade of blue on your laptop screen.

Find four things you can feel.

The weight of your watch. The texture of your jeans against your leg. The slight coldness of the table under your hand.

Find three things you can hear.

The distant siren. The click of the keyboard. The refrigerator hum.

Find two things you can smell.

Find one thing you can taste.

Do this quickly. Do not linger. You are forcing the executive function of your brain to work on objective reality. The mind cannot simultaneously calculate the catastrophe of 2027 and catalogue the scent of stale coffee. It is a rapid cognitive bottleneck. Use it.

TACTIC 2: THE TEMPERATURE SHOCK RESET

YOUR NERVOUS SYSTEM IS DESIGNED TO RESPOND IMMEDIATELY TO sudden changes in temperature. Anxiety is a high-revving engine. The fastest way to slow it down is to signal to the body that there is a more immediate, physical priority than the internal noise.

This is why people splash water on their face during a panic attack. It works.

You don't need a bucket of ice. You need a fast, sharp change.

Keep a bottle of ice-cold water nearby. When the spiral hits, put the bottle directly against your wrist pulse point, or hold it pressed to the soft skin on the side of your neck.

The shock of the cold is a massive sensory input. It forces the system to re-route energy. It bypasses the abstract thinking and engages the immediate physical senses.

You can also carry a small, smooth, cold stone or even a chilled coin in your pocket. Clench it when you feel the surge. That sharp, tangible coldness is your physical anchor. It doesn't solve the problem, but it pulls you out of the mental theatre where the problem is being rehearsed.

TACTIC 3: THE FOOT LOCK

Anxiety often feels like you are floating away. Like you are disconnected from your body and the physical world. Your brain is traveling faster than your feet.

You need to re-engage gravity.

When you feel the noise rising, consciously drive your feet into the floor.

Push down. Hard.

Imagine you are trying to lift a thousand-pound weight using only the pressure between your feet and the ground. Feel the pressure in your soles, your calves, the muscles around your hips.

Focus one hundred percent on the sensation of that physical resistance.

This is not a stretch. It is a forceful, physical grounding exercise. It literally locks you into the territory you occupy. It tells your brain: I am here. I am connected to the ground. Gravity is real. The threat is abstract.

The mind is a powerful engine. But the body is a powerful anchor. Use these tools not for gentle reflection, but for immediate, tactical interruption.

They are the code's fire alarm. Fast. Simple. Effective. And they don't require you to believe in anything except basic human neurology.

THE 3 NON-NEGOTIABLE TACTICS THAT INSTANTLY INTERRUPT A DEEP OVERTHINKING SPIRAL

When the spiral hits, it feels like an internal hostage situation.

Your brain has locked onto a catastrophic loop.

It's running a movie you've seen a hundred times before.

It feels productive.

It feels necessary.

It is absolutely, 100% consuming your energy and achieving nothing.

You need an emergency, physical interrupt.

You cannot think your way out of a thought spiral.

You must act your way out.

These three tactics are non-negotiable.

You do them instantly.

You do them aggressively.

They are designed to bypass the thinking brain entirely.

TACTIC 1: THE PHYSIOLOGICAL SHOCK (THE TEMPERATURE DROP)

When you are deep in the spiral, your body is in high alert.

Your heart rate is up.

Your stress hormones are flowing.

You must introduce an external, immediate physiological demand that overrides the internal noise.

We are shocking the system back to the present.

The fastest way to do this is temperature.

Stop whatever you are doing.

Walk immediately to the sink.

Turn the tap to the coldest setting possible.

Cup the water.

Dunk your face into the cold water for a count of three seconds.

If you are wearing makeup or cannot wet your face, take a handful of ice cubes.

Press them firmly to the back of your neck or directly onto your wrists.

The intense cold forces your brain to register physical reality.

It triggers the dive reflex, which instantly lowers your heart rate.

The overthinking process stops because the brain has been given a new, clear, immediate priority: I am cold.

It works every single time.

TACTIC 2: THE COGNITIVE CALLOUT (THE LABELLING METHOD)

The spiral maintains power because you believe the content is urgent and real.

You are fully merged with the idea.

The goal here is instant defusion.

We break the merger by identifying the process, not the content.

As soon as you notice the loop, stop internally engaging the thoughts.

Do not try to argue with them.

Do not try to solve the problem they are presenting.

Instead, label the internal mechanism out loud.

Say: "I am running the Rehashing That Embarrassing Meeting loop right now."

Or: "This is the Worry Forecast Model 7 simulation."

You can even add a quick tag: "Ah, that's the Inner Critic trying to scare me again."

The key is to use the label to externalize the thought.

By naming the process, you separate yourself from the voice.

You are the observer noticing the noise.

You are not the noise itself.

This simple act of identification pulls your attention out of the mental movie and into the role of the director.

It strips the thought of its authority.

TACTIC 3: THE BEHAVIORAL ANCHOR (THE FIVE-MINUTE RULE)

OVERTHINKING IS OFTEN A HIGHLY SOPHISTICATED FORM OF procrastination.

You are afraid of the task or the decision, so you hide in planning and worrying.

The only way out is immediate, small, productive action.

The action must be measurable.

It must have a definite start and stop.

Commit to just five minutes of simple, physical movement or task completion.

Not related to the core worry.

Clear your desk.

Load the washing machine.

Go outside and walk exactly 100 steps.

The rule is: Start the small task, commit to five minutes, and allow the thinking spiral to continue in the background.

You are not fighting the thoughts.

You are just refusing to give them the exclusive right to your body's time.

Movement generates momentum.

When the five minutes is up, you will have broken the inertia.

The completion of a small task provides a micro-dose of confidence and capability.

It proves to your system that you are not paralyzed.

This immediate, small win usually deflates the catastrophic tension enough for the rest of the noise to dissipate naturally.

Use these three tools interchangeably.

They are your emergency interrupt button.

They demand action.

They refuse engagement.

They guarantee a pause.

CHAPTER FOUR

The Control Illusion: How Trying to Steer the Uncontrollable Drains 80% of Your Daily Energy

You are tired.

Truly, deeply, bone tired.

This specific flavor of exhaustion isn't physical.

It's mental fatigue.

It's the heavy, weighted blanket feeling of perpetual vigilance.

You feel like you are paddling a tiny plastic kayak.

Right in the middle of a global hurricane.

And you are clutching the paddle so hard.

White knuckles.

Eyes wide open.

Ready to steer everything.

The economy.

Your spouse's mood.

The stock market.

The traffic on the I-95.

The past argument you had five years ago.

The exact timeline of your upcoming illness.

The collective political fate of the western world.

This is the Control Illusion.

It is the belief that if you just think hard enough.

If you just worry well enough.

If you formulate the perfect 17-step contingency plan for an event that has a 2% chance of occurring.

You can steer the uncontrollable.

This illusion is the single greatest energy sink in the modern human experience.

It is a black hole for your mental reserves.

We spend 80% of our daily battery life right here.

Trying to move immovable mountains.

Why do we do this?

Because uncertainty feels like danger.

To the ancient brain, control equals safety.

The caveman could control his spear. His fire. His immediate surroundings.

Control was directly correlated with survival.

Your brain still runs that ancient software.

It screams: Find the danger! Fix the danger! Control the outcome!

But your dangers now are abstract.

They are market forces. They are other people's opinions. They are the unpredictable randomness of life.

These things cannot be fixed by worrying.

They are simply outside the perimeter of your influence.

Your anxiety is not a warning sign of actual danger most of the time.

It is the internal alarm system going off.

Because the brain detects too many variables it cannot influence.

It desperately tries to create order through obsessive thought.

It substitutes rumination for actual agency.

It tells you: "If you stop worrying, you stop caring."

That is the biggest lie the Control Illusion tells you.

The noise is the sound of your mental gears grinding against reality.

It is the futile resistance to what simply is.

You need a perimeter check.

This is the blunt, immediate truth that sets you free.

It's a foundational stone of psychological peace.

The ancient Stoics figured this out two thousand years ago.

They called it the Discipline of Assent, or simply, the Dichotomy of Control.

Draw a circle.

Inside the circle is everything you genuinely control.

Your effort.

Your integrity.

Your response to an event.

Your chosen values.

Your decision to start swimming or stay paralyzed.

Outside the circle is everything else.

Other people's thoughts about you.

The outcome of your project.

The weather.

The past.

Future outcomes.

The noise you are hearing right now?

It's the sound of your brain hammering frantically at the walls of that perimeter.

Trying to expand the circle.

Trying to drag the uncontrollable back inside.

It never works. It just exhausts the carpenter.

Think about the effort you waste.

We try to steer the past.

We rerun conversations in the middle of the night.

"If only I had said that clever thing."

"If only I hadn't agreed to that meeting."

This is time travel for masochists.

It changes nothing.

It steals your current reality.

You are pouring energy into a bucket with no bottom.

We try to steer the future.

We worry about five possible scenarios that might unfold in five years.

We plan the perfect rebuttal to an argument that hasn't happened yet.

We pre-suffer.

Pre-suffering is just the cost of trying to control what isn't available yet.

The future is an outcome.

You can influence the inputs right now.

But you cannot control the outcome itself.

The result belongs outside the circle.

And then there are people.

This is the Control Illusion at its most toxic and exhausting.

We spend so much time managing others.

We try to manage their perceptions of us.

We carefully edit ourselves in real time.

We try to manage their moods. Their decisions. Their appreciation of our hard work.

This is a fool's errand built on sand.

You can inspire. You can influence.

You can communicate your truth clearly.

You absolutely cannot control their internal state or their subsequent choices.

When they are unhappy, that is their weather system.

It is not your duty to chase away their clouds.

You are not the weatherman. You are just standing nearby.

Stop trying to change the forecast for everyone around you.

It is exhausting. It is intrusive. And it will destroy your peace every time.

The moment you recognize: This is not mine to steer.

That is the moment the rope slackens.

The great misunderstanding is that peace equals surrender.

That acceptance is weakness.

That letting go means you stop caring or stop trying.

It is the exact opposite.

Radical acceptance is strategic intelligence.

It is an aggressive, energy-conserving strategic choice.

It means you look at the uncontrollable storm—the recession, the difficult client, the health scare, the inevitable human fallibility—and you decide:

I will not waste my limited fuel fighting the wind.

I will acknowledge the reality of the storm.

I will drop the anchor.

And I will focus every ounce of effort on what is still mine.

My action. My integrity. My next step.

This is the fastest way to regain mental freedom.

It releases monumental energy.

The energy you were previously using to power the illusion of control.

When the anxiety hits—that feeling of overwhelming responsibility—stop.

Ask the hard, blunt question:

Is this truly within my control?

The answer will be almost always: No.

Is my boss going to respect my boundary? Maybe. I control the setting of the boundary.

Is this project going to succeed? Maybe. I control the quality of my work.

Is my difficult relative going to finally change their behaviour? No. I control how I respond to their behaviour.

The power doesn't sit in the outcome.

It sits solely in the input.

When you refuse to try and grab the rudder of the universe, two things happen immediately:

First, your mental bandwidth expands.

Suddenly, you have energy back.

You can apply that 80% drain toward constructive action within your circle.

You can plan your work instead of planning your worry.

You can be present in a conversation instead of rehearsing the next five moves.

Second, the panic deflates.

The pressure of responsibility—the idea that if you just tried harder, you could stop bad things from happening—evaporates.

You realize you were carrying a load that was never yours to bear.

This is the difference between struggling violently against a current that will crush you.

And turning slightly to swim with the current, only focusing on staying afloat.

You are still swimming. You are still acting.

But the useless resistance is gone.

You stop trying to win the war against reality.

When you practice this, your brain will scream betrayal.

It will interpret this acceptance as laziness.

It will say: "You are giving up!"

Remind it gently: "No. I am finally choosing to focus my efforts where they matter."

Acceptance is not passive resignation.

It is the most efficient choice available.

It is a choice to engage with reality as it is, not as you desperately wish it to be.

This stops the struggle.

And stopping the struggle is how you turn the volume down on the perpetual noise.

It is how you plug the biggest leak in your energy tank.

Drop the heavy burden.

You don't have to steer the ocean.

You just have to steer yourself.

DISCOVERED: THE SIMPLE CATEGORIZATION SYSTEM THAT RELEASES 90% OF YOUR STRESS IMMEDIATELY

We spend 80% of our mental energy every single day fighting gravity.

We are arguing with forces that do not care about our opinions. We are trying to push against the tide. We are attempting to negotiate with the past.

It is pointless. It is exhausting. It is the core mechanism of almost all chronic stress.

We need a way to stop this fight. Not through endless meditation. Not through positive thinking. We stop it by installing a clean, logical filter in our minds. A system that identifies the targets we can actually hit.

This is not theory. This is a surgical tool.

It is a two-part classification system. When you identify a point of stress—any thought that steals your breath, any fear that makes your hands clammy—you force it into one of these two categories.

Category 1: The Circle of Influence.

Category 2: The Ocean of the Uncontrollable.

The goal is to stop treating the ocean as if you can steer it with your bare hands.

Let's define them ruthlessly.

The Circle of Influence (Category 1) is tiny. It contains only four things:

1. Your Effort Today.
2. Your Attitude (Your interpretation of events).
3. Your Preparation (Your planning and actions).
4. Your Response (How you react to a result).

That's it. That is your entire jurisdiction.

The Ocean of the Uncontrollable (Category 2) is vast. It contains everything else.

Other people's opinions of you.

The economy next year.

The outcome of a job interview you already finished.

The weather.

The traffic.

The decision your boss will make.

Everything that happened yesterday.

When you feel anxiety spike, your only job is to perform a diagnostic check.

Ask yourself: Does this worry fall within the four items in the Circle of Influence?

If the answer is yes, you stop worrying and start moving. You convert the thought into immediate action.

If the answer is no—and it will be no 90% of the time—you must practice immediate, unconditional release.

This is the stress hack. The immediate release of worry about the uncontrollable is why the system works so fast. You are not trying to fix the problem; you are deciding whether the problem even belongs to you.

Imagine you are driving and are stuck in unexpected traffic.

The Malfunctioning Brain: This is going to make me late. Everyone is going to judge me. Why didn't I leave earlier? This is unfair.

This is Fusion. You are trying to influence the flow of two thousand cars moving around you. You are trying to influence the internal judgment of your boss. You are failing. You are burning energy.

The Code-Oriented Brain: Wait. Is the traffic in my Circle of Influence? No. Is my reaction? Yes.

The noise stops.

What changes? You change your focus. You focus on the one thing you can control: your response. You use the extra time to listen to a helpful podcast. You send a quick, neutral text message. You adjust your breathing.

The traffic problem does not vanish, but the stress about the traffic problem—the secondary layer of panic, the frantic attempt to steer the unsteerable—instantly drops to zero.

That is 90% of the stress released immediately.

We confuse concern with control. We think that because we are concerned, we must possess the power to alter the situation. This is a tragic psychological error.

You can be concerned about a friend's job loss. You can love them. You can offer help. But you cannot make them send out new applications. Their effort belongs to their circle. Your support belongs to yours.

If you are spending five hours ruminating on something that belongs squarely in the Ocean of the Uncontrollable, you are draining your life force for absolutely zero return. You are committing a futility crime against your own nervous system.

Clarity is the ultimate power tool. When you are clear about the limits of your power, you stop attacking walls that refuse to move, and you start building doors in the places where you actually have jurisdiction.

The first step toward peace is not feeling calm. The first step toward peace is knowing exactly what you are allowed to touch.

Sort the thoughts. Draw the line. Release the rest. Do it now.

THE FUTILITY TRAP: WHY WISHING THINGS WERE DIFFERENT IS A GUARANTEED PATH TO SUFFERING AND EXHAUSTION

You know the feeling of true, deep exhaustion. It is not physical fatigue. It is the depletion of the soul.

This exhaustion is caused by one thing. It is the effort required to argue with reality.

You hate the current situation. You wish it were different. You spend mental energy trying to undo the past. You try to force a different present. This effort is what we call the Futility Trap. It is a guaranteed path to suffering. It guarantees complete exhaustion.

Stop wishing the thing hadn't happened. It did happen.

Stop wishing the market hadn't crashed. It did crash.

Stop wishing that conversation went differently. It is over now.

The past is a permanent, fixed event. Wishing changes nothing about the facts. It only chains your mind to what you cannot change. You are demanding a different outcome from a settled event. This is the definition of mental friction. You are fighting the structure of time itself. You will lose this fight every time.

Then there is the trap of other people.

You desperately want someone to apologize. You want your spouse to understand your pain. You want your boss to recognize your effort. You want your family to behave maturely.

Stop it. You have zero control here.

You cannot manage other people's thoughts. You cannot force their emotions. You cannot dictate their actions. People are sovereign nations. They operate on their own messy logic.

You spend vast amounts of energy trying to steer them. You try to manipulate the environment. You construct elaborate scenarios in your mind to justify their change. You try to reason the unreasoned. This effort is the greatest drain on your mental battery.

Trying to control another person's behaviour is always an act of violence against yourself. You tie your peace to their unpredictability. This guarantees anxiety. This guarantees resentment.

The futility of this effort is absolute.

You cannot make someone see the truth. You cannot force understanding. You can only communicate your truth. Then you must release the outcome.

Every hour you spend wishing your friend was more supportive is an hour wasted. Every moment you spend demanding your partner be less stressed is a moment of self-imposed tension.

Accept this profound limitation. You can only control your own action. You can only control your response. You can only manage your effort. That is the limit of your sphere of power.

Release the wish for the perfect apology. Release the demand for perfect understanding. Release the need for things to be fair.

When you drop the rope in the tug-of-war against reality, you are suddenly free. This is not surrender. It is strategic conservation. You are reclaiming the 80% of energy you waste on impossible goals.

Reality is heavy. You cannot lift it. Stop trying. Recognize what is true right now. Start from there. That is the only escape hatch from the trap.

RADICAL ACCEPTANCE: WHY 'GIVING UP' IS ACTUALLY THE MOST AGGRESSIVE, ENERGY-CONSERVING STRATEGIC CHOICE YOU CAN MAKE

We have to talk about the word "acceptance."

It is the dirtiest word in the self-help lexicon.

It sounds weak. It sounds passive. It sounds like throwing in the towel, sighing deeply, and just giving up on your goals.

I promise you, nothing could be further from the truth.

If you are a driven person—and I know you are, or you wouldn't be reading this—you view resistance as virtue. You view struggle as necessary. You believe that fighting what is undesirable is how you succeed.

But there is a specific category of fighting that is not heroic. It is stupid. It is devastatingly expensive.

That fighting is resisting reality.

Radical acceptance is not liking the situation. It's not agreeing with the situation. It is simply stating: "This thing is true right now."

The difference between a strategic choice and a psychological death spiral is defined entirely by this single point.

Think about the sheer, wasted energy of wishing. Wishing that the market hadn't crashed. Wishing that awful person hadn't behaved that way. Wishing that the accident hadn't happened five years ago.

That internal monologue of "If only..." is a massive, constant drain. It is you running your engine at 8,000 RPM while stuck in neutral. You are burning fuel. You are generating heat. You are creating noise. But you are not moving an inch.

The market crashed. That person behaved badly. The accident happened.

Arguing with these facts is arguing with history. History does not care about your argument. The event is complete.

When you practice radical acceptance, you make the most aggressive, energy-conserving move possible. You refuse to waste one more joule of mental effort on trying to mentally undo what is already done.

This is the ultimate redirection of resources.

When you refuse to accept reality, you are constantly applying pressure against a closed door. That pressure requires energy. That energy creates anxiety and rumination.

When you radically accept reality—when you stand up, look at the door, and say, "Okay, the door is closed, and my history is what it is"—you instantly release that pressure.

The immediate outcome is not weakness. The immediate outcome is a surge of available energy. It is a decisive, tactical shift.

You are not giving up on making things better. You are giving up on the fight against the terrain.

It's the difference between the general who argues with the map because he doesn't like the mountains, and the general who instantly accepts the mountains and pivots his army around them.

The first general gets stuck and starves. The second general wins the campaign.

Radical acceptance is the moment you transition from the helpless victim of the past to the aggressive architect of the future. It forces you to ask the only question that matters: Now what?

It eliminates the "Why me?" pity party that is so comfortable, yet so costly.

We often confuse acceptance with resignation. Resignation says, "I guess I'll just live with this terrible feeling forever."

Acceptance says, "I accept that this terrible situation is true right now, and because I accept that truth, I am no longer spending energy fighting it. All that energy is now free to build a better life starting in the next five seconds."

This is the most aggressive mental state available to you.

It means refusing to be a prisoner of circumstance. It means declaring sovereignty over your internal resources. It means saying to the noise, "I acknowledge you, but I will not engage in your pointless fight."

It is the ultimate energy hack. It is the refusal to pay the psychological interest on debts that have already been settled.

Stop arguing with the facts of your life. Accept the temperature of the room. Accept the bad behavior of others. Accept the truth of your bank account.

Do not like it. Do not endorse it. Just acknowledge its presence.

In that fierce, honest acknowledgement, you reclaim your power. You instantly liberate 80% of the mental energy you were wasting on resistance.

That is how you start building. That is how you conserve your strength for the things that truly matter. That is not surrender. That is profound strategic superiority.

THE HIGH-LEVERAGE AREAS: REDIRECTING CONTROL ENERGY TO PRODUCTIVE SELF-IMPROVEMENT (THE 10X ROI FRAMEWORK)

You just created an energy surplus.

You released your grip on the vast, indifferent universe.

That panic. That need to forecast every tragedy. That demand for perfect outcomes. That was taking up 80% of your operational bandwidth. That energy is now free.

It is a massive windfall.

The critical next step is strategic investment. You cannot just let that energy pool and stagnate, or it will immediately revert to noise. It will find something new to worry about.

Instead, we redirect it. We channel that fierce desire for control into the very few areas where control actually exists.

This is the 10x ROI Framework. We want maximum return on our mental investment. We stop polishing the rusty external things. We focus only on sharpening the internal mechanisms.

Where does the worried brain want to go? It wants to fix global politics. It wants to change your boss's personality. It wants to reverse time.

Where must the high-leverage energy go?

It must go here.

THE HIGH-LEVERAGE AREA 1: YOUR BIOLOGY BASELINE

The most profound, most overlooked area of control is your own physical engine. When the brain is loud, the body is usually screaming, too.

Your chronic overthinking guarantees poor sleep. Poor sleep guarantees mental instability. Your coffee reliance guarantees adrenaline crashes.

You cannot think your way into peace if your body is running on gasoline fumes.

The 10x ROI on physical control is instant. Better sleep is instant thought defusion. Consistent movement is instant anxiety discharge. Proper fuel stabilizes blood sugar, which stabilizes mood.

Ask yourself: Am I using my control energy to worry about macroeconomics, or am I directing it to make sure I drink enough water and go to bed at a predictable hour?

Focus your control impulse on sleep hygiene. On nutrition intake. On the 20 minutes of daily physical effort you owe your stress system.

This is 100% within your sphere of influence. This is where control pays dividends.

THE HIGH-LEVERAGE AREA 2: THE CORE COMPETENCE STACK

A MASSIVE SOURCE OF WORRY IS ROOTED IN PERCEIVED INADEQUACY. Do I have enough money? Am I good enough at my job? Will I be okay if everything falls apart?

You cannot control the economy. You cannot control your industry's next downturn.

But you absolutely control your core skill stack.

Your control energy should be redirected from forecasting doom to building armor. Worrying about your job security is low-leverage. Spending thirty minutes every day learning a new, marketable skill is 10x ROI.

Worrying about a potential financial disaster is exhausting. Building a small side income stream is empowering.

Take the energy you used to rehearse future failure. Reinvest it in mastering the present skill. When you feel competent, the internal noise about inadequacy shrinks instantly. Action cures this kind of fear. Worry does not.

THE HIGH-LEVERAGE AREA 3: ENVIRONMENTAL STANDARDS AND BOUNDARIES

We expend tremendous energy trying to manage the feelings and reactions of other people. This is zero-leverage. Trying to control how your mother-in-law perceives you? Trying to ensure your co-worker delivers on time? Futile.

But you have absolute control over your environment and the standards you set within it.

You redirect the energy from controlling others to controlling your walls.

This means mastering the non-negotiable "No." This is aggressive self-protection. Saying "No" to a social obligation frees up hours of energy you would have spent anticipating the conflict.

It means establishing clear communication walls with difficult people. You cannot change their reaction, but you can change your participation. You control the duration of the conversation. You control the information you share. You control the time you allow for their chaos.

The moment you redirect that energy from managing their expectations to enforcing your own boundaries, you get peace back.

It is a ruthless, disciplined trade.

Stop trying to manage the outcome of a meeting you already finished.

Start aggressively controlling the inputs of your life: your body, your skills, and your walls.

This is what stoicism means by moving from passive acceptance to active effort. We are not just giving up the control illusion; we are strategically relocating that control energy into high-yield self-improvement. The difference is measurable. The return is guaranteed.

CHAPTER FIVE

—★-★-★—

The Noise Cancellation Hack: Practical Techniques for Quieting Emotional Reactions Without Toxic Suppression

YOU HATE FEELING THINGS DEEPLY.

Let's be honest.

You don't want peace because you love stillness. You want peace because you are tired of the constant, searing heat of your own emotional reactions.

The anger flares up.

The fear paralyzes you.

The shame crashes down without warning.

And every time, you think: I need to stop this. I need to get rid of this feeling. I need to push it down so I can function.

That is the lie that guarantees chaos.

That is the suppression trap.

We confuse true emotional mastery with emotional deafness. We think quieting the noise means killing the messenger. We think strength means feeling nothing.

Toxic suppression is the act of pretending a feeling doesn't exist. You shove it deep into your mental basement, lock the door, and then spend all your energy sitting on the lid, terrified it might burst open.

It always bursts open.

It doesn't vanish. It doesn't dissolve. It just transmutes into something uglier: chronic fatigue, random bursts of passive aggression, or that tight, immovable knot in your shoulders that no massage can fix.

The goal of emotional regulation is not to achieve the state of a Zen master who smiles beatifically at tragedy. The goal is to become permeable.

We want to allow the wave to pass through the shore, rather than trying to build a wall against the ocean.

This chapter is the manual for that process. It is the Noise Cancellation Hack. It allows you to hear the sound of the siren without merging with the frequency. It allows you to feel the deep, ugly, necessary truth of your current emotion without letting it dictate your behaviour, ruin your week, or destroy your relationship.

It demands processing, not ignoring.

It starts with an essential recognition.

The feeling is not the fact.

The feeling is an internal message. It is a biological data point. But in the moment of intensity, we become fused with the feeling. We believe the feeling is the whole reality.

The feeling of panic makes the entire world feel dangerous.

The feeling of shame makes us believe we are inherently worthless.

We forget that it is just a chemical bath. We forget that it is energy.

You need to learn how to deal with the energy before the mind can weave the destructive story around it. If you try to argue with the story while the energy is still searing hot, you lose every time.

You must handle the heat first.

The first step in noise cancellation is locating the signal.

We are so good at talking about our feelings—talking around them, arguing about them, intellectualizing them—that we forget to actually locate them in the body.

The emotional experience is fundamentally somatic. It happens in the flesh. It happens in your organs.

The thoughts are just the loud, messy interpretation of that physical sensation.

Stop asking, "Why am I so anxious?"

Start asking, "Where is the anxiety living right now?"

This is the physical pivot. This is the radical grounding that overrides the screaming committee.

When the anxiety hits, it is loud. It demands your full attention. It demands a story. It demands action. It needs you to pick up the phone and text the person who annoyed you. It needs you to catastrophize your retirement fund.

Don't give it the narrative fuel.

Just locate it.

The fear lives as a buzzing in my palms. The shame is a lead weight behind my breastbone. The frustration is fire behind my eyes.

When you identify it as physical data—as a tingling, a tightness, a heat—you immediately strip away its psychological power. It stops being an existential crisis and starts being a physiological event.

And physiological events can be managed. They can be moved.

Your mind is a brilliant, terrifying storyteller. But your body is simple. Your body responds to gravity, breath, and temperature.

When you locate the feeling in the body, you can then apply physics to it. You are moving from the messy realm of philosophy back into the predictable realm of biology.

This is the core difference between processing and suppression.

Suppression says: Ignore the tight chest.

Processing says: Acknowledge the tight chest. Breathe into it. Feel the tightness, knowing it is temporary. Allow the sensation to be exactly what it is.

This is not passive surrender. This is strategic, objective observation.

You must understand the chemistry of intensity.

Dr. Jill Bolte Taylor, the neuroanatomist, famously stated that the chemical lifespan of a pure, unadulterated emotion—the rush of adrenaline, the cortisol release—lasts only ninety seconds.

Ninety seconds.

That is the wave. The peak and the crash.

If you are angry for an hour, or anxious for three days, you are not experiencing the original, pure emotion anymore. You are experiencing the loop.

You are reliving the initial 90-second chemical dump, and then your brain is instantly restarting the timer by feeding you fresh narrative fuel.

This is where the noise comes from.

"You're right to be angry," the inner voice says. "Remember how disrespectful they were last Tuesday? And what about that time three years ago when your old boss pulled the same trick? This is a pattern. You must fight."

And boom. You are chemically back at minute zero.

The Noise Cancellation Hack here is learning to survive the 90 seconds without adding the narrative.

When the feeling hits—the sudden, overwhelming dread—you need to implement the micro-pause.

Stop everything.

Just for a moment.

Don't run. Don't scroll. Don't lash out.

Say, "I am feeling X." Use a precise word if you can: rage, terror, intense sadness.

Then, commit to observing the feeling without movement for 90 seconds.

This is incredibly hard. Every nerve ending will scream at you to do something. The anxiety wants you to panic. The guilt wants you to confess something you didn't do. The jealousy wants you to check their phone.

Your job is simply to hold still and let the chemical storm rage inside its 90-second container.

You breathe. You locate the sensation. You observe the heat, the tremor, the shortness of breath.

When you do this, you are effectively running interference on the brain's ability to restart the loop. You are separating the pure signal from the toxic noise.

You are saying, "I hear the distress, but I am refusing the narrative that justifies perpetual distress."

This is emotional courage. True courage is not denying the fear. True courage is feeling the fear, giving it the 90 seconds it deserves, and then choosing your next action from a place of biological cooling, not chemical urgency.

The noise cancellation hack also involves physical techniques for discharge. We'll get into the somatic secrets later, but understand this now: Emotions are stored kinetic energy.

Rage is locked-up fight energy.

Fear is locked-up flight energy.

If you feel intense emotion and just sit there trying to meditate it away, you are creating a pressure cooker. The energy needs a non-destructive outlet.

When you feel overwhelming frustration—the type that makes your teeth ache—you don't need to talk about your childhood trauma. You need to physically move the energy.

You need to disrupt the internal pattern.

You need to step away from the desk. Shake your hands vigorously for thirty seconds. Do ten deep, loud exhales. Go run up and down the stairs twice.

This is not a distraction. This is a physiological reboot.

You are telling your nervous system: "I recognize the fight response you initiated, but we don't need it right now. I am consciously discharging the adrenaline so we can shift back to safety."

When you handle the physical energy of the emotion, the mental noise automatically drops. The committee starts whispering instead of screaming.

This approach—locating, allowing the 90-second wave, and discharging—is the exact opposite of suppression. Suppression is passive. This is active, conscious engagement with your inner chaos.

It is how we learn to quiet the reaction without killing the feeling.

Because ultimately, we don't want to kill the feeling. Feelings give life color. They tell us when boundaries have been crossed. They tell us when we need change.

We just want to stop them from making us functionally useless. We want to stop the reaction from becoming the reality.

We want noise cancellation. We are turning the volume down so we can finally hear the signal, instead of just the static.

★ ★ ★

THE 'FINE' LIE: MOVING PAST GENERIC STRESS TO PRECISE EMOTIONAL IDENTIFICATION (THE CLARITY HACK THAT ENABLES MANAGEMENT)

WE NEED TO TALK ABOUT THE 'F' WORD.

Not the fun one. The damaging one.

Fine.

How are you? Fine. How is work? Fine. How is your escalating sense of existential dread? Oh, I'm fine.

"Fine" is a linguistic surrender. It is the sound of your brain slamming the door shut on honest observation. It is a defense mechanism built out of exhaustion.

Why do we resort to it?

Because precision feels dangerous. It means commitment. It means we have to actually deal with the thing.

The same is true for the slightly more sophisticated, yet equally useless, label: Stressed.

You feel stressed. Okay. That is like calling your car trouble "broken." It tells the mechanic nothing. Is it the engine? The flat tire? The radio volume?

If you walk around telling yourself, "I am stressed," your brain hears a loud, confusing alert. It registers global danger. It screams, but it can't locate the fire.

It becomes chronic, unfocused noise.

The secret to emotional management is almost absurdly simple. It's clarity.

Clarity is the ultimate hack.

The management of complex psychological states requires surgical precision, not a broad-spectrum antibiotic. You cannot fix what you cannot define. You can only define what you can separate.

Think of your emotional state like a bundle of knotted wires. If they're all stuck together and you label the bundle ANXIETY, you can't find the short circuit. You just have to scream at the whole mess.

What we must do is become meticulous emotional taxonomists. We have to pull the wires apart.

The key question is not, "How stressed am I?"

The useful, power-generating question is: "What specific emotion is fueling this noise?"

We need to trade the blunt instrument of "stress" for the sharp scalpel of truth.

It is almost never just "stress."

Often, that feeling you call stress is actually resentment. Resentment that you said yes when you desperately wanted to say no. Resentment that you are carrying someone else's burden.

Often, that low hum of anxiety is shame. Shame about something you did last week. Shame about something you feel unqualified to handle.

Often, that feeling of dread is grief. Grief for a former life, a lost opportunity, or a relationship that is fundamentally different now.

Notice the fundamental shift in power.

If I tell you, "I feel stressed," you give me a lavender bath bomb.

If I tell myself, "I feel deep resentment because I agreed to manage this project when I am already overloaded," I know exactly what tool to use. The solution is not mindfulness. The solution is boundary-setting. The solution is a difficult conversation.

If I tell myself, "I feel anxiety," the noise continues.

If I tell myself, "I feel fear of inadequacy regarding next Tuesday's presentation," the brain can then engage the problem-solving function: Prepare slides. Rehearse. Seek coaching.

The feeling shrinks from a global threat into a specific, addressable task.

This is the power of precision. This is why we move past "fine."

Every time you precisely label an internal experience—I am frustrated. I am lonely. I am envious. I am overwhelmed by the volume of emails—you immediately create space. You separate the self from the noise.

It's like taking a monster that was shapeless and ten feet tall, and shrinking it down to a labeled, manageable box on a shelf.

Once it's a box, you can decide whether to open it, file it, or throw it away.

But first, you have to read the label.

Stop being polite to your pain. Stop generalizing your suffering. Be specific. Be brutally honest. That honesty is the absolute prerequisite for management.

Name it precisely. Manage it effectively.

SHOCKING DISTINCTION: HOW TO PROCESS DEEP PAIN WITHOUT FALLING INTO CYCLES OF VICTIMHOOD OR RUMINATION

Deep pain is not the problem.

The problem is what we do with the pain.

Most people confuse endless cycling with deep work. They think if they feel bad long enough, they are somehow solving the issue.

They are not. They are just running the memory on repeat.

We need a powerful distinction here.

There is processing.

And there is punishing yourself with the past.

Processing is clean. It is acute. It has a goal.

When you process pain, you feel the feeling. You allow the grief to move. You recognize the rage. You give the emotion its 15 minutes of fame.

The goal of processing is integration. It is discharge.

It looks like crying until you are empty. It looks like writing the necessary letter and then tearing it up.

It focuses on the present reality of the loss. It drives you toward a future where that loss is incorporated.

It is about the feeling.

It is always time-limited.

Rumination is the opposite.

Rumination is sticky. It is chronic. It is perpetual.

The goal of rumination is to re-prove the injustice. It is recycling the facts to find a new angle of suffering.

It never solves anything. It just keeps the wound raw.

It is about the story.

Victimhood takes it one step further. It takes that raw story and fuses it to your identity.

When pain is processed, it is an event that happened to you.

When pain turns to victimhood, it becomes who you are.

I am a victim of this betrayal. I am a person who was wronged.

This fusion is catastrophic.

Why?

Because if the identity is wrapped up in the pain, you are required to keep the pain alive to maintain the identity.

You become incentivized to hold onto the suffering.

The moment you let go of the pain, you risk losing the story. You risk losing the sympathetic audience. You risk losing the narrative that defined you.

That is why victimhood is the ultimate trap. It turns healing into self-betrayal.

The key distinction is this:

Healthy Processing: Focuses on the internal emotion and the action you can take now. It asks, "What do I need to feel?" and "What is my next move?"

Unhealthy Cycling (Rumination/Victimhood): Focuses on external details and the actions others took. It asks, "Why did this happen to me?" and "How can I prove I was mistreated?"

Check your output.

If you are rehashing the specific texts, the specific tone of voice, the specific date of the argument—that's rumination. You are seeking justice in the details, which is impossible.

If the telling of your pain requires an immediate, specific reaction from the listener—sympathy, outrage, validation—that's victimhood. You are seeking emotional payment.

Processing feels draining but cleansing.

Cycling feels draining and exhausting.

Choose cleansing. Feel the pain. Let it move. Discharge it.

Do not let the pain become your permanent address.

The pain deserves respect. It deserves to be felt.

It does not deserve to be the permanent center of your world.

Separate the wound from the identity.

That separation is where freedom begins.

EXPOSED: THE SOMATIC SECRET OF ANXIETY (3 SIMPLE PHYSICAL WAYS TO DISCHARGE EMOTIONAL TENSION IN UNDER 60 SECONDS)

YOU HAVE SPENT SO MUCH TIME TRYING TO THINK YOUR WAY OUT OF anxiety.

You've tried to analyse the thought.

You've tried to challenge the belief.

You have tried to be logical with the screaming committee.

And it failed because you missed the critical secret.

The anxiety isn't just in your mind. It is stored energy.

It is physical debt.

Anxiety, at its core, is a somatic experience. It is the physiological residue of a fight-or-flight response that never got to fire. You got the adrenaline dump. You got the cortisol surge. But since you couldn't punch your boss or run away from the mortgage payment, that energy got trapped.

Where does it go?

Your jaw. Your neck. Your diaphragm. Your lower back.

The chronic tension you carry is the body's way of keeping that explosive energy suppressed. You are spending massive amounts of physical energy holding yourself together.

We must stop treating anxiety as a purely mental disorder. It is a full-body state of alert. If you want true, rapid calm, you must discharge the physical fuel.

We need physical reset buttons. Not affirmations.

Here are three simple, zero-cost, physical ways to discharge trapped emotional tension in under sixty seconds. They are crude. They are fast. They work.

1. THE INTENTIONAL SHAKEOUT (20 SECONDS)

Think about how mammals handle trauma. A gazelle gets chased by a lion and escapes. What does it do immediately afterward? It doesn't sit down to process its feelings. It trembles violently. It shakes off the residual adrenaline.

We, as humans, suppress this natural response. We try to be polite. We try to be still. This is why we hold tension.

This technique is simple: You need to let your body vibrate.

Stand up, if you can. If you can't, do this sitting down. Shake your hands and arms rapidly, like you are trying to fling water off your fingertips. Jiggle your legs. Let your jaw hang loose and shake your head slightly side to side.

Look ridiculous. Feel the vibration moving through your core. This is not mindful movement. This is intentional somatic discharge. Do this for twenty seconds. It tells your nervous system: The danger is gone. We are safe to shake it off.

It is a powerful, instant circuit breaker for the fight response.

2. THE VAGUS NERVE HUM (30 SECONDS)

The Vagus nerve is the main communication line between your brain and your major organs. It is the express route for regulating your parasympathetic nervous system—your rest and digest system.

When you stimulate the Vagus nerve, you send an undeniable signal of calm to your entire body. We can do this with sound.

Take a slow, deep breath into your belly. Not your chest. Deep.

Now, as you exhale, make a loud, sustained humming sound. HMMMMMMMM.

Make it deep and audible. Feel the vibration resonating in your chest cavity, throat, and skull. The key is the length and depth of the exhale, and the resonance of the sound.

Do three full cycles. Inhale slow. Exhale loud and long with the hum.

This is a physical, mechanical action that forces your heart rate to slow down. It calms the system from the inside out. It takes thirty seconds, and it is a reliable physiological anchor.

3. THE 10-SECOND CLENCH-DROP (15 SECONDS)

THIS TECHNIQUE USES THE CONTRAST PRINCIPLE TO RESET MUSCLE tension.

When you are spiraling, your muscles are subconsciously flexed, ready for action. You might not even realize your shoulders are up near your ears.

You are going to intentionally amplify that tension and then crash it to zero.

Sit or stand. Take one deep breath.

Now, hold your breath and simultaneously tense every single muscle group you can access. Clench your fists until your knuckles are white. Flex your arms. Tighten your core. Squeeze your legs together. Make your face tense.

Hold that maximal tension for 10 full seconds. Hard. Uncomfortable.

Then, with a loud, audible sigh or groan, drop every single muscle instantly. Let your arms fall limp. Let your jaw slacken.

The immediate contrast between maximal tension and total release sends a clear physical signal: The action is over. The system is offline.

You cannot hold anxiety effectively in a limp, relaxed body. This method forces a moment of total physical surrender.

These three methods are not about changing your thoughts. They are about changing the state of your central nervous system. When the body stands down, the brain naturally gets quieter.

Use them when the noise gets too loud. Use them before you reach for the phone. Use them before you try to argue with the thought.

Discharge the energy first. Then, look at the thought. The noise will sound profoundly less threatening once the physical fuel has been drained.

THE MICRO-PAUSE SYSTEM: 5 HIGH-IMPACT, 90-SECOND BREAKS THAT PREVENT TOTAL EMOTIONAL OVERWHELM DURING A WORKDAY

THE BIGGEST LIE WE TELL OURSELVES DURING A STRESSFUL DAY IS, "I can push through."

You cannot push through emotional overwhelm.

It's not a muscle you train.

It is an energy system that fails.

Most of us wait until the red line. We wait until the laptop is slammed shut and we are hiding under the desk. That's too late. The damage is done.

The secret to preventing total emotional breakdown during a workday is pre-emptive interruption. You need to hit the reset button before the smoke alarm goes off fully.

You don't need a 30-minute yoga session.

You need 90 seconds.

This is the Micro-Pause System. These are small, tactical shifts you can execute at your desk, in the bathroom stall, or while waiting for coffee. They pull you out of the emotional spiral and ground you, fast.

Here are five high-impact, 90-second breaks.

1. THE TEMPERATURE CHECK (90 SECONDS)

WHEN THE NOISE STARTS CHURNING, THE GOAL IS TO SHIFT YOUR focus from internal rumination to external, physical sensation.

Stop staring at the screen.

Pick up a cold glass of water or a coffee mug. Notice the temperature on your hand. Really feel it.

Stand up. Push your feet into the floor. Notice the pressure. How does the sole of your shoe feel?

Look around the room. Name five things you see that are not digital. A wall. A pen. A plant.

You are forcing the high-alert brain to report on the immediate, harmless environment. This grounds you in reality, not scenario-planning.

2. THE THREE-THOUGHT TRIAGE (60 SECONDS)

Your brain is shouting multiple, competing demands. We tend to merge with all of them, believing they are equally urgent and important.

Take a quick breath. Do not close your eyes. Look down at your hands.

Ask: What are the three loudest thoughts in my head right now?

Write them down mentally or physically.

A: I need to call the client back. (Actionable)

B: I am terrible at this job. (Judgment)

C: My sister hasn't texted me back. (Uncontrollable Worry)

See them. Label them by category: Action, Judgment, Worry.

Do not try to solve them. You simply acknowledge their existence. This acts as immediate defusion. You've seen the thoughts. Now put them back on the shelf.

3. THE SHOULDER DUMP (90 SECONDS)

Anxiety and cognitive overload live physically in your neck, shoulders, and chest. The body is always ready to run. You have to discharge that latent tension.

This is a physical reset.

Pull your shoulders up as high as they can go, trying to touch your ears. Squeeze hard. Hold for ten counts. Feel the tightness.

Then, forcefully exhale and drop them. Not gently. Dump them. Let them fall.

Repeat this three times. Pull high, hold, dump hard.

The physical release of tension sends a powerful signal to the nervous system: The threat is gone. You are safe enough to relax your armor.

4. THE UNCONTROLLED INVENTORY (45 SECONDS)

THIS IS YOUR INSTANT STOIC CHECK, STRAIGHT FROM CHAPTER 4.

You are feeling overwhelmed because you are worried about things that are not yet real, or things that are entirely outside your influence.

In 45 seconds, mentally review your immediate crisis point.

Is this about something I did five minutes ago? (Yes/No)

Is this about something someone else might do in the future? (Yes/No)

Can I literally, physically, execute the solution to this problem in the next ten minutes? (Yes/No)

If the answer is No to the last question, or Yes to the second question, you must mentally file it under "Not My Lever."

Release the tension. Recognize the futility of holding onto that specific thread of control. You can't steer other people's decisions right now. You can't edit yesterday's email.

5. THE NEXT-ACTION ANCHOR (30 SECONDS)

THE WORST THING TO DO AFTER A RESET IS TO PLUNGE BACK INTO the chaos without direction. Emotional overwhelm often stems from a massive, vague to-do list looming over you.

This micro-pause forces granular focus.

Define your Anchor.

Not, "I need to finish the Peterson Report."

That is too big. That feels heavy.

Define the smallest possible, single next step.

"Open the Peterson folder."

"Write the subject line for the email."

"Read the first paragraph of the instructions."

Anchor yourself to that tiny, achievable action.

When the 30 seconds are up, you don't engage with the list. You just execute the Anchor. This uses the fresh, quiet mental space productively and prevents the spiral from starting again.

Use these Micro-Pauses five times a day. Use them proactively, like maintenance. Use them immediately when you feel the noise volume creep up. Don't wait until the smoke alarm turns into a house fire. Stop the cycle, 90 seconds at a time.

CHAPTER SIX

—★-★-★—

MEET THE COMMITTEE: An Inventory of the Voices Driving You Mad (And How to Get Them to Shut Up)

Your brain is not a quiet library.

It is a chaotic committee room.

It's the worst corporate board meeting you have ever attended. Loud. Unstructured. Everyone shouting over everyone else. And the worst part? The people with the loudest, dumbest opinions usually run the show.

They run you.

You have spent years listening to this internal committee as if their pronouncements were sacred scripture. Every screech of panic. Every prediction of doom. Every analysis of your profound inadequacy. You accepted it as the ultimate truth of who you are.

But they aren't you. They are just employees. Employees who have gone severely rogue.

This chapter is the inventory. Before we can fire them or, more gently, demote them, we have to meet them. We have to identify their distinct voices, their roles, and their absolutely terrible motivations. When you can name the voice, you stop merging with it.

You create distance.

Distance is power.

Let's pull back the curtain on this dysfunctional group that lives rent-free in your skull.

THE INNER CRITIC: THE JUDGE

You know this one best. He's the loudest member of the committee. He's the one with the gavel and the permanent scowl.

The Inner Critic operates on one core principle: Perfection is the only acceptable baseline.

He doesn't care about effort. He cares only about outcome. And if the outcome is less than perfect, he has a 14-point summary of why you are inherently flawed.

This voice is deeply cruel. It speaks in absolutes: "You always mess this up." "You never finish anything." "Everyone else is managing, why aren't you?"

We grant this voice authority because it sounds like it knows what it's talking about. It uses specific evidence from your past. It points to failures. It feels deeply familiar.

And that familiarity is the trap.

Think about the tone. Is it constructive? Does it sound like a loving mentor? No. It sounds like a prosecutor. It uses shame as its primary motivational tool.

Shame is not a motivator. Shame is a paralyzer.

The Judge demands constant vigilance and self-punishment. If you try to relax, he points out all the tasks you haven't completed. If you achieve something, he immediately pivots to the next, higher standard.

His job is to keep you small by keeping you perpetually guilty.

The key to dealing with The Judge is realizing his intentions are outdated. He likely formed when you were a child, copying the harsh voice of an external authority (parent, teacher, society) in an attempt to keep you safe from external judgment.

He was a misguided protector. Now he's just a bully with tenure.

THE PARANOID PLANNER: THE FORECASTER

THIS IS THE VOICE OF PURE ANXIETY. IT OFTEN TRIES TO MASQUERADE as productivity.

The Paranoid Planner is obsessed with the future, but not the hopeful, exciting future. Only the disastrous one.

His job is to run worst-case scenarios—all of them, simultaneously.

If you have a big presentation next week, The Forecaster doesn't help you rehearse slides. He forces you to visualize forgetting your pants, tripping over the cable, and the resulting humiliation leading to your eventual homelessness.

He thinks that by pre-suffering, you are somehow prepared.

This is the ultimate lie of anxiety.

Worrying does not prevent bad outcomes. It only prevents you from enjoying the present moment.

The Forecaster is the most exhausting committee member because he never sleeps. He forces you to mentally rehearse arguments that haven't happened, anticipate illnesses that haven't manifested, and structure finances around fictional collapses.

He convinces you that if you stop worrying, you'll be blindsided.

But here is the truth of The Forecaster: his analysis is always based on imagination, not data. His predictions are rarely 100% accurate, yet you treat them as 100% gospel.

How do you spot him? He uses language like, "What if..." "But we should consider..." "If this fails, then..."

The moment you catch yourself spending mental energy on a scenario that has less than a 5% probability of happening within the next 24 hours, you have found The Forecaster.

He needs to be put on permanent, mandatory vacation.

THE TASKMASTER: THE INNER DIRECTOR

THE TASKMASTER IS THE VOICE OF RELENTLESS, AGGRESSIVE optimization.

He is not necessarily mean, but he is utterly tireless and compassionless. He turns your entire life into a checklist.

He is responsible for your productivity guilt.

You just finished a successful project? The Taskmaster is already shouting: "Good. Now what's next? You wasted 15 minutes checking your phone. We could have been optimizing."

He fears stillness. He hates gaps in the schedule. Rest is seen as a flaw in the system. Leisure is a failure of planning.

When you try to relax, The Taskmaster pops up with a nagging sense of obligation. You feel itchy. You feel like you should be doing something else.

He turns every enjoyable activity into a high-stakes performance. Are you relaxing correctly? Are you fully present during this leisure activity?

Even your mindfulness practice becomes a performance review under the Taskmaster's scrutiny.

The result of his reign is chronic burnout. You feel permanently behind schedule, regardless of how much you achieve. You mistake frantic activity for actual progress.

Recognize the Taskmaster when you feel physical tension creeping in during quiet moments. He's the one whispering, "You're wasting time."

He needs a strict, permanent schedule that includes mandatory, non-negotiable breaks. He hates rules, but he responds to clear structure.

THE SHAMER: THE ARCHIVIST OF MISTAKES

THE SHAMER LIVES IN THE PAST. HIS OFFICE IS FILLED WITH FILING cabinets labeled "Regrets," "Embarrassments," and "Missed Opportunities."

While the Critic focuses on inherent character flaws, The Shamer focuses on specific historical events. He is the master of the mental flashback.

He loves 3:00 AM. That's his prime time.

He drags out that awkward thing you said at the party five years ago. He replays the fight you had with your sister in slow motion. He makes you feel the hot flush of shame all over again, even though the event is over and resolved.

Why does he do this? Because he equates remembering pain with learning a lesson.

He believes if you forget the severity of the mistake, you are destined to repeat it. So, he keeps the wound fresh.

The Shamer is the voice that says, "I can't believe you did that."

He forces you to ruminate—to chew the same emotional cud over and over until you are raw. Rumination is suffering the same event multiple times.

He needs to be stopped because he steals two things crucial for peace: acceptance and forward motion. You cannot move forward if someone is constantly pulling you backward by your old mistakes.

The Archivist's power relies on your willingness to engage with the ghosts he summons. If you refuse to look at his files, they gather dust.

THE DYSFUNCTIONAL BOARDROOM

THE TRUE CHAOS OF YOUR BRAIN HAPPENS WHEN THESE FOUR—THE Judge, The Forecaster, The Taskmaster, and The Shamer—all start arguing at once.

The Judge says you are a failure.

The Forecaster panics about the financial ruin that failure will cause next month.

The Shamer reminds you of the similar failure you had in college.

The Taskmaster demands you stop sitting there and start doing something pointless right now to fix a non-existent problem.

It's exhausting. It's overwhelming. It's paralyzing.

But look what we just did. We gave them names. We described their tactics. We noticed that they have distinct, predictable, and frankly, ridiculous personalities.

None of those descriptions sound like the calm, rational, capable person reading this book.

This is the power of externalization.

As long as you say, "I am anxious," The Forecaster has won. You have merged with his voice.

But when you can say, "The Paranoid Planner is screaming about financial ruin again," you shift.

You are no longer the panic. You are the observer of the panic.

This separation is the foundational key to turning down the volume. They can scream all they want, but the moment you stop believing they are the CEO of your life, they lose executive authority.

Their thoughts become just noise.

When the committee meets, your only job is to recognize who is speaking and how utterly unqualified they are to manage your peace. We don't try to silence them yet—that's suppression, and it backfires.

First, we identify them. We catalog their ridiculous scripts. We know their favorite lies.

We understand their job is to create discomfort, either through fear of the future or shame about the past, and to demand constant, frenetic effort.

But they have operated in the shadows long enough. Now the lights are on. We know their names.

And once you know the identity of the monster, it stops being quite so scary. It just becomes a tedious, repetitive pain in the neck.

Now we are ready to rewrite the scripts. We are ready to stop giving them the mic.

THE PERSONA LIST: IDENTIFYING AND NAMING YOUR INNER DIRECTOR, YOUR OVERBEARING CRITIC, AND YOUR PARANOID PLANNER

THE NOISE IS EXHAUSTING BECAUSE YOU THINK IT'S ONE LOUD voice.

It is not.

It's a committee.

A messy, badly organized, consistently frantic committee. They all want the microphone at the same time.

And they all sound exactly like you.

This is the trick. This is cognitive fusion. Because the thought sounds like your internal monologue, you assume the thought is your central identity, your truth, your objective self.

It is not.

Your internal voices are just internal roles. They are scripts you learned long ago. They are outdated operating programs that run on autopilot.

You are the CEO. They are the managers.

And we are going to name them right now. Naming them is the first step in taking away their power. You cannot argue with "anxiety." You can argue with a guy named "Gary."

When you hear a destructive thought, you need to be able to tag it instantly. This thought belongs to The Planner. This thought belongs to The Critic.

Here are the three most common, loudest members of the committee.

The Overbearing Critic

This is the voice that is truly unkind.

It uses definitive, damning language. It uses words like always and never.

"You always mess this up."

"You never finish what you start."

"You are fundamentally incapable."

It doesn't just critique your actions; it attacks your character.

Why does it do this? Because, misguided as it is, The Critic is trying to protect you. It learned a long time ago that if it humiliates you first, if it sets the bar so high that you never dare to try, then you can't fail publicly. It thinks shame is a motivational tool. It believes if you are miserable enough, you will avoid future pain.

It's wrong. It's deeply wrong. But that's its twisted motivation.

We need to hear that voice and say, "Thank you for your input, Critic. Your assessment is noted and declined."

The Paranoid Planner

This voice lives 48 hours into the future. Always.

It is constantly running catastrophe simulations. It's obsessed with the "What if" scenarios.

You are planning dinner, and The Planner is already calculating the budget deficit of the next fiscal quarter. You are enjoying a quiet evening, and The Planner is drafting your resignation letter just in case the entire industry collapses.

This voice is the ultimate risk assessor. Its motivation is simple: preemptive control. If it can imagine every single disaster, it believes it can stop it.

The Planner creates a massive inventory of imaginary problems that require immediate action, drawing down your energy reserves and preventing you from being effective right now.

The Planner is why you feel tired before you even start the day. Because The Planner has already made you live through Tuesday's tragedy.

When this voice surfaces, you need to recognize its signature: it's always based on fiction, not fact. It's built on hypotheticals, not the present moment.

The Inner Director

The Director is concerned with appearance.

This is the voice that obsesses over the social script. It replays conversations from yesterday, scrutinizing every nuance.

Did I use the right tone?

Did that person notice my hesitation?

I should have said X instead of Y.

Rehearse the perfect response for the impossible conversation you might have tomorrow.

The Director is convinced that if you deviate from the perfect, polished script, you will be exposed. It is the keeper of your public image, and it is a tyrant.

Its motivation is social acceptance and perceived flawless performance. It wants you to be liked and respected by everyone, which is an impossible, exhausting goal.

The Director is why you feel performing in your own life.

Naming The Committee

These three, or variations of them, are the ones burning down your mental house.

Now you have identified their specific roles and their misguided motivations.

The key to defusion is personalization. Give them names. Silly names. Distant names.

Maybe your Critic is "Chad." He's a terrible manager who peaked in high school.

Maybe your Planner is "Patty," an obsessive accountant who can't handle uncertainty.

Maybe your Director is "Doris," a theater major who critiques your breathing.

When Chad pipes up and says, "You're going to fail," you don't absorb that as truth.

You simply hear, "Ah, Chad is talking again."

It creates an immediate, non-negotiable distance. It reminds you that the voice is an occurrence—a script playing out—not your identity.

It's just a noise. A character in a play you are currently choosing not to watch. And you are holding the remote.

Turn the volume down on Chad. Tell Patty you'll review the budget later. Tell Doris to relax.

You don't have to engage with the committee just because they scheduled a meeting in your head.

★ ★ ★

THE MISGUIDED PROTECTOR: TRACING THE DEVELOPMENTAL ROOTS OF YOUR INNER CRITIC (HINT: IT WAS ONLY TRYING TO HELP, BUT FAILED)

WE SPEND SO MUCH ENERGY TRYING TO KILL THE INNER CRITIC.

We fight it. We negotiate with it. We curse it out.

And it just screams louder.

The truth is, you can't kill it because it isn't a monster.

It is a misguided protector.

It has the best, most terrifying intentions.

To understand it, you have to trace its roots back to the moment you were smallest. When you were most vulnerable.

Think about childhood.

The world was vast. It was confusing. You needed connection to survive. Acceptance was currency. Rejection was a physical threat.

You learned very quickly that certain behaviors led to pain. Maybe shame. Maybe isolation.

Your brain, the incredible problem-solving machine we discussed, started creating preemptive defenses.

If I anticipate the external threat, maybe it won't hit so hard.

If I catch my own mistakes first, maybe the important people won't punish me.

The Critic was born in this gap. It was your internal security system, built to prevent outside pain by administering internal pain first.

It was designed to keep you compliant. To keep you safe. To keep you small enough and quiet enough to remain a member of the tribe.

It worked.

For that small child, the inner criticism truly was a necessary, though painful, tool for navigating an unpredictable world. It was a shield made of fear. It helped that version of you survive.

And then it got stuck.

That voice never updated its operating system.

It is still running on the assumption that you are five years old. It still believes that a minor mistake at work will lead to social rejection that threatens your very existence. It maintains that level of emergency.

It is an ancient, loud, and ineffective alarm system.

It still thinks that yelling at you—calling you stupid, or lazy, or a failure—will somehow motivate you or protect you from a worse fate.

It doesn't understand that now, its volume is the only thing causing you suffering.

It is the security guard who tackles you when you try to walk through your own front door.

So, the first act of defusion isn't hostility. It is gentle, compassionate diagnosis.

We acknowledge the origin.

We see that fear is fueling the engine. The voice isn't criticizing because it hates you; it's criticizing because it is terrified that if you drop your guard for one second, something terrible will happen.

This distinction is massive.

When you recognize the Critic as a scared, outdated child-protector, it loses its adult authority. You stop treating it like a supreme judge. You start treating it like a well-meaning relative who needs to retire.

You do not need to fight the fear itself. You need to acknowledge it.

Look at the thought that says, "You are going to fail this presentation."

You look deeper and ask, "What is the fear behind this?"

The answer is usually: "I am afraid of shame/rejection/looking incompetent."

And then you can gently remind the old protector: That was a real threat once. But I am an adult now. I have new tools. We can handle a bad presentation. We do not need to panic.

You are replacing the old, aggressive defense mechanism with the calm authority of your adult self.

You are taking the keys away from the tired, overreacting guard.

You don't need to scream. You just need to say, with clarity and kindness: Thank you for trying. But you are fired. I've got this now.

THE TOXIC SCRIPT DECODER: RECOGNIZING THE CRITIC'S FAVORITE PHRASES ('YOU ALWAYS MESS THIS UP') TO INSTANTLY WEAKEN ITS NARRATIVE POWER

THE INNER CRITIC IS NOT A GENIUS.

It is boring.

It uses the same five toxic scripts, over and over again, for every failure, every worry, and every moment of doubt. It has no fresh material. It just runs the same worn-out program, changing only the names and dates.

This predictability is your ultimate weapon.

The instant you recognize that the thought you are having is not a fresh, original insight but a tired, recycled narrative—a script—you gain distance. You stop treating it as a profound truth. You treat it as what it is: canned, automatic dialogue.

When you can name the type of thought, you stop responding to the content. You start responding to the pattern. That is where the power immediately drains out.

Let's decode the Critic's greatest hits. This is the Toxic Script Decoder.

SCRIPT 1: THE ABSOLUTE LIE (THE "ALWAYS/NEVER" SCRIPT)

The Critic loves absolutes. It deals only in generalizations.

The Phrases:

"You always mess this up."

"You are never going to succeed."

"No one ever listens to you."

"This will permanently define you."

What it does: This script denies every single past success or exception to the rule. Its sole purpose is to induce paralyzing hopelessness, making the current problem seem universal and terminal. The Critic knows if you feel hopeless, you stop trying.

Your response: When you hear the words "always" or "never," your internal red flag must fly high. They are guaranteed falsehoods. Label it: There's the Absolute Lie script.

SCRIPT 2: THE CORE IDENTITY ATTACK

This script is the cruellest because it shifts focus from the action to the self.

The Phrases:

"You are fundamentally broken."

"You are unlovable."

"You are stupid/weak/worthless."

"This proves you are not worthy."

What it does: It targets your identity, making the problem feel internal and unfixable. If you made a mistake on a spreadsheet, the Critic doesn't say, "Fix the spreadsheet." It says, "You are a total idiot and should not be trusted with numbers." It seeks to define your entire being by one isolated incident.

Your response: Recognize this as the attempt to move from doing to being. Label it: This is the Core Identity Attack. Rejected.

SCRIPT 3: THE FORTUNE TELLER CATASTROPHE

THE ANXIOUS BRAIN INSISTS IT KNOWS THE FUTURE, AND THAT FUTURE is always terrible.

The Phrases:

"This is going to be a disaster."

"When they find out, you'll be ruined."

"What if X happens, and then Y happens, and then Z happens, and I lose everything?" (The chain reaction of doom.)

What it does: The Critic insists on forecasting the worst possible outcome, often using vague, dramatic language. It attempts to load you with responsibility for imaginary, future events that are completely outside your control. This is the definition of unproductive rumination.

Your response: If the thought begins with "What if..." and ends with "total ruin," it's the Fortune Teller script. Simply say: I don't take advice from fortune tellers.

SCRIPT 4: THE COMPARISON TRAP

COMPARISON IS THE THIEF OF JOY, AND YOUR CRITIC LOVES thievery.

The Phrases:

"Everyone else is handling this better."

"Your friend/neighbor/coworker is 10 years ahead of you."

"You are so far behind."

What it does: This script forces you into a false comparison based on partial, curated information. It compares your honest, messy internal reality (your current fear, your failures, your true struggles) with someone else's highlight reel or, worse, with an idealized version of yourself that doesn't exist. It ignores context entirely.

Your response: Label it: Ah, the Comparison Trap. We are only comparing me to who I was yesterday.

The Shift from Message to Script

The difference between suffering and peace often comes down to this single move.

When a toxic thought hits, you must intercept the initial impulse to agree with the message and instead identify the script.

Look at the difference:

Situation: You forget a deadline.

The Fused (Suffering) Reaction: I am so incompetent. I always drop the ball. I'm going to lose my job because I can't handle simple tasks. I should just give up. (You believe the message.)

The Defused (Code) Reaction: I hear the Absolute Lie script telling me I always drop the ball. And there's the Core Identity Attack saying I should give up. Interesting. Now, what is the next actual step? (You label the script.)

This small act is massive.

By labeling the script, you automatically shift the thought from the category of "Truth" to the category of "Psychological Event."

The goal is not to stop the Critic from talking. It will talk. It's part of your noisy brain.

The goal is to stop granting it authority.

We don't argue with the script. We don't debate the facts it presents. We just file it away: Toxic Script 4: Comparison.

When you see the pattern, you see the lie. The narrative power collapses. It turns from a personal, devastating attack into predictable, automated background noise. We don't need to shut the committee up entirely. We just need to stop listening to their horrible advice.

—★–★–★—

THE COMFORT OF FAMILIAR PAIN: WHY WE GRANT AUTHORITY TO THE VOICE THAT CAUSES US THE MOST SUFFERING

THIS IS THE WILDEST PART OF THE WHOLE MENTAL GAME.

We grant authority to the voice that hurts us most.

We listen to the Critic. We allow it to berate us. It points out flaws in stunning, repetitive detail. It screams about future failures. And we sit there, nodding. We say, "Yes. That sounds right. That sounds like me."

Why do we believe the committee member who is openly hostile?

Why do we choose to grant the podium to the speaker who guarantees our misery?

Because it is familiar.

It is the oldest soundtrack in your operating system. That critic, that worrier, that constant fault-finder—it has been running the show since childhood.

Maybe it started as a parental echo. Maybe it was a survival mechanism you developed in school. Whatever the origin, that voice has been running the show for decades.

It is a known quantity.

Familiarity breeds a toxic type of trust. Even if that voice delivers pain, it delivers predictable pain. You know exactly what misery it will serve up for breakfast. You can set your watch by the flavor of the self-doubt.

It is consistent.

Now, contrast that with peace.

Calm is unfamiliar territory. Silence feels like a void.

The anxious, primitive brain is designed for vigilance. It thinks: If I stop worrying, I stop preparing. If I stop listening to the Critic, I might become complacent. I might miss the danger.

The deep psychological trap is this: Suffering equals Vigilance equals Safety.

The brain interprets the absence of noise not as peace, but as a dangerous lack of preparation.

To step off the treadmill of familiar self-abuse feels profoundly risky. It feels like taking the hands off the wheel, even though the wheel has been steering you into walls for years.

The Critic offers certainty. It is a terrible certainty, yes. "You are definitely going to fail at this job." "You are definitely unlovable." This is a solid statement. It is a known quantity.

The alternative—the possibility of calm, the quiet observation of reality—is the unknown.

The human system is fundamentally wired to prefer the known path, even if that path is covered in sharp stones. We trade peace for predictability. We trade potential joy for the false security of habitual pain.

This is the comfort of familiar pain. It is the rut your emotional tires run in. It is deep. It is easy to follow. It requires zero conscious effort.

You must realize that the authority you give this voice is a habit, not a necessity. You do not need to earn peace by first suffering. You do not need to pay the pain tax.

That voice is an unreliable narrator. It is a broken smoke alarm.

Stop giving it the microphone. Stop granting it the keys to the kingdom just because it's the oldest one in the room. You have the power to mute it. You just haven't exercised that power yet. You mistook its longevity for its legitimacy.

It has neither.

The silence you seek is not scary. It is merely new. And it is waiting.

CHAPTER SEVEN

★-★-★

The Voice Training Protocol: Actively Cultivating the Calm, Objective Inner Narrator in 14 Days

WE HAVE COVERED A LOT OF GROUND.

We identified the noise.

We practiced not believing the noise.

We categorized the chaos.

Now comes the work. The active training. The real shift.

This is the Voice Training Protocol. It is the conscious, persistent effort to replace the malfunctioning smoke alarm with a calm, capable CEO.

It won't happen by accident. You can observe the anxious voice all day long, but observation alone is passive. It gives you peace in the moment. But to build sustainable peace, you must build muscle memory. You must actively recruit and train a new, better voice.

Think of it like learning a new language. You start by just listening. That's Chapters 1 through 6. You recognize the sounds. You understand the grammar of the chaos. Now, you have to start speaking the new language. You will sound clumsy. You will stumble. It will feel forced and fake.

Good. That means it's working.

Your brain has been speaking the language of panic, urgency, and catastrophe for years. That wiring is deep. We are laying new fiber optic cables right next to the rusted copper wires of the old system.

The 14-Day Protocol is the framework for that install. Don't obsess over the 14 days. It's not a magic cure deadline. It is a period of intense focus designed to break the automaticity of the old voice. It's enough time for the new, calmer script to feel less like a performance and more like a habit.

The fundamental shift we are making is from subject to observer, and then from observer to objective narrator.

The anxious voice says: I am overwhelmed.

The objective voice says: I am currently experiencing a sensation of overwhelm. I have three tasks due. I can choose one to start now.

Notice the difference. It's subtle, but seismic. The anxious voice is the experience. The objective voice reports the experience and then immediately looks for the next actionable step. This is the definition of Stoic mental hygiene. It is clean. It is efficient. It is boring.

And boring is exactly what we are aiming for.

Boring means peace.

Understanding the Calibration of the New Voice

The CEO voice has two primary characteristics: low volume and slow cadence.

Your anxious voice is a screaming headline in all caps. It uses exclamation points. It is urgent. It demands immediate, total attention. It sounds like a frantic personal conversation happening in your chest.

Your objective narrator is a flat, fact-based memo delivered in a monotone. It sits in your frontal lobe. It never uses emotional language. It never uses absolute terms like "always," "never," or "ruined."

You need to train yourself to hear the difference in acoustic quality. When you catch the old voice starting, don't just defuse the thought. Defuse the volume.

Lower the internal volume.

Slow the internal pace.

This physical act of slowing down the mental speech pattern is a powerful circuit breaker. The feeling of urgency is chemically tied to the speed of your internal monologue. Speed up the monologue, you speed up the adrenaline. Slow it down, you give the chemistry time to dissipate.

The Protocol: The Daily Rewrite

Your task for the next 14 days is simple but non-negotiable: You must actively rewrite the toxic script every time you catch it.

This is not optional. This is the rep count.

We start by using the three tools of the objective narrator:

1. Identification without Judgment

2. Present-Moment Assessment

3. The Immediate Next Step

Here is how the Daily Rewrite works:

Scenario: You are checking email on Monday morning. You see a confusing request from your boss.

The Old Voice (The Critic/Paranoid Planner) instantly fires up.

OLD VOICE: Oh my god, this is confusing. I don't understand this at all. I must look incompetent. I'm going to mess this up, they are going to know I can't handle this job, and then I'm going to lose my career. This is totally overwhelming.

Stop. Take one breath. This is where you activate the CEO.

The New Voice (The Objective Narrator) steps in.

NEW VOICE: I am having a strong thought that I will lose my job. That thought is based on one confusing email. I currently feel pressure in my chest. What is the observable fact? The fact is, I received an email containing three specific questions (A, B, C). I don't immediately know the answer to C. This is not a catastrophe. This is a problem to be solved. What is the immediate next step? The immediate next step is to reread the email slowly and highlight A, B, and C.

You see what happened?

We took a trajectory that went from one email to career destruction and we short-circuited it back to the desk.

This is the constant practice. You are catching the exaggeration and forcing it into the harness of measurable reality.

The Critical Role of Low-Stakes Practice

You will not successfully deploy the objective voice when you are in a major argument or facing a massive financial crisis on Day 3. The noise is too loud.

We start small. We practice in the most mundane, low-stakes environments. You are building mastery through predictability.

Example Practice Areas for Days 1-7:

Traffic: The old voice screams that the other drivers are idiots, that you will be late, and that this delay proves the universe is against you.

The new voice says: I am stationary. The estimated delay is seven minutes. I can use this time to adjust my posture. The noise is not relevant to my safety.

Spilled Coffee: The old voice rages about the waste, the inconvenience, and your general clumsiness. It uses shame as fuel.

The new voice says: Coffee has spilled. I need three paper towels. The action required is cleanup. The feeling is minor irritation. This event has zero long-term consequence.

A Small Unmet Expectation: You planned to get X done, but only got Y done. The old voice immediately begins the self-flagellation.

The new voice says: I completed 70% of the planned tasks. My expectation of 100% was perhaps unrealistic for the time allowed. I will shift the remaining 30% to tomorrow's list.

Every successful deployment of the new voice is a deposit into your mental bank account. These tiny wins program your brain to default to peace. They prove that the calm voice is competent and effective.

The new voice doesn't offer false hope. It offers utility.

The 14-Day Accountability Structure

To maintain the necessary intensity for 14 days, you need an accountability method. You can't just rely on wishing.

I recommend the "Three Capture" method.

Every day, you must capture at least three instances where the old voice tried to take over, and you successfully performed the Daily Rewrite.

Get a small notebook or use a note app. Label the entry:

1. Trigger (The confusing email, the traffic jam, the messy kitchen).
2. Old Script (The catastrophe narrative).
3. New Script (The objective, action-oriented, flat response).

This written record is vital. It creates immediate physical evidence that the old script is merely a suggestion, not a reality. It shows your brain the pattern of failure and then immediately gives it the blueprint for success.

When you look back at the end of 14 days, you will see twenty-one examples of successful thought substitution. That evidence is undeniable. It breaks the illusion that you are powerless against the noise.

The Danger of Waiting for Motivation

This is the hardest part of the protocol: You have to do the work when you don't feel like it.

We wait for motivation to hit us like a lightning bolt. It rarely does. We wait for the moment we feel "calm enough" to deploy the objective voice.

That's a trap.

The objective voice is not generated by calm. It is what creates calm. It is the action, not the result.

When the anxiety peaks, the urge is to merge with the feeling, to solve the crisis the old voice has manufactured. This is when the discipline matters most.

You must interrupt the spiral with two phrases:

1. Stop. (A quick, sharp, internal command.)
2. What is fact? (The immediate pivot to objectivity.)

You are actively refusing to grant the screaming committee the authority of the CEO. You are simply stating: Your input is noted. It is based on emotion, not data. I am going a different way.

This is an aggressive stance. It is not passive self-care. It is a psychological counter-attack.

Persistence Over Perfection

You will fail. You will have days where the old voice runs rampant, and hours later, you realize you spent the entire afternoon in a destructive loop about something entirely outside your control.

This is not a setback. This is data.

The objective narrator does not judge failure; it analyzes it.

If you miss a full day of practicing the rewrite, the CEO voice does not say: You ruined your 14 days. You always mess this up. Why bother continuing?

No. The CEO voice says: I missed the practice yesterday. The consequence was heightened anxiety. The plan for today is to recommit to the Three Capture method immediately.

The protocol isn't about achieving a zero-anxiety state in 14 days. It is about establishing the habit of interruption and substitution in 14 days. It is about proving to your own operating system that there is a better default setting available.

The power of this protocol lies entirely in consistency. It doesn't matter if you have a perfect rewrite every time. It matters that you try three times, every single day, for two weeks.

This is how you lay the foundation for permanent change. You are training the muscle that chooses peace. You are cultivating a voice that you can trust. A voice that is not dramatic, not panicked, and not based on the past.

A voice that simply asks: What is true, and what is the next productive step?

Listen for that voice. It is already there. We just need to turn its volume up.

WHY NEUTRALITY BEATS POSITIVITY: SHIFTING YOUR NARRATOR FROM HARSH JUDGE TO OBJECTIVE OBSERVER (NO 'FLUFFY' AFFIRMATIONS REQUIRED)

WE ARE DONE WITH TOXIC POSITIVITY.

We are done with fluffy affirmations that feel like a lie when you say them out loud.

You know the drill. They tell you to look in the mirror. You are supposed to scream, "I am a successful, vibrant, financially abundant human being!"

But your brain knows the truth. It sees the stack of bills. It remembers the mistake you made yesterday.

Your inner Critic doesn't get quiet when you use aggressive positivity. It gets louder. It counter-attacks. It says, "Oh yeah? Prove it, liar."

The internal civil war ramps up.

Toxic positivity is fundamentally a form of intellectual denial. It is trying to force a fake reality onto a messy, inconvenient one.

This never, ever works for sustainable peace.

What we need is not positivity. What we need is neutrality.

Neutrality is the silent superpower. It is the core operational shift we need to install in our system.

You are not training your narrator to be a cheerleader. You are training your narrator to be a court reporter.

The court reporter just writes down the facts. They don't add emotion. They don't add judgment.

Imagine the difference in processing data.

The Critic (The Judge) says: "I am pathetic for not having finished that project on time. I'm a terrible professional."

That judgment fuses with your identity. You become the pathetic, terrible professional. You shut down.

The Objective Observer (The Neutral Narrator) says: "I notice the project deadline passed yesterday. The consequence is I now have X amount of catch-up work to do."

Do you see the distinction?

The Neutral Narrator reports on the external event and the internal state without assigning moral failure. It simply registers the data.

There is no emotional fuel in data.

There is only fuel in judgment.

When you judge yourself, you merge with the thought. You collapse the distance. You give the thought the power to define you.

When you observe the thought neutrally, you keep the distance. You remain the quiet operating system, watching the thoughts scroll by.

You are the person observing that you are stressed. You are not the stress itself.

The moment you can describe your experience factually, without emotion, you deflate the entire panic cycle.

This is why we reject the positive affirmation approach. If the Critic says, "You are a failure," and you aggressively counter with, "No, I am a brilliant success," you are still engaged in the fight. You are still granting the Critic authority by arguing with it.

The power of neutrality is that it doesn't argue. It acknowledges the noise and downgrades its status.

Let's practice the downgrade.

Your brain screams: "I am going to lose everything." (Judgment/Forecast)

The Neutral Narrator responds: "I notice a strong feeling of financial fear has just arrived. The thought states that I am going to lose everything."

Your brain screams: "Why can't I stop thinking about what I said five years ago?" (Judgment/Shame)

The Neutral Narrator responds: "My memory system is currently replaying a socially awkward event from five years ago. I am experiencing a powerful sense of heat and discomfort."

You are simply labeling the content. You are documenting the occurrence of the noise.

You are not fighting the wave. You are just saying, "Oh, look, a wave."

The transformation is in the language you use internally. You must eliminate adjectives that carry moral weight (lazy, pathetic, brilliant, amazing). You replace them with measurable states (resistant, tired, achieved goal X, completed task Y).

The Neutral Narrator is the ultimate reality checker. It forces you to stop engaging with fiction (the Critic's hyperbolic judgments) and start engaging with data (the actual situation).

This shift pulls your focus away from the vague, overwhelming anxiety and redirects it to the micro-level task that you can actually control right now.

You train yourself to speak the cold, hard, non-emotional truth about your inner world.

You stop giving the judge the microphone. You hand it to the reporter instead.

This quiet, objective voice is what we are cultivating over the next fourteen days. It requires no spiritual fluff. It only requires ruthless honesty and distance.

THE STOIC INSTANT-SHIFT PROMPTS: SIMPLE QUESTIONS (LIKE 'WHAT CAN I DO RIGHT NOW?') THAT STOP PANIC DEAD

PANIC IS FAST.

It is an electrical surge of feeling demanding an immediate, massive solution.

The overthinking brain—the Malfunctioning Smoke Alarm—gets loud when it thinks a problem is too big to solve. It demands complete clarity before it will quiet down.

That is why trying to calm yourself with vague affirmations never works. "I am safe" means nothing when your internal system is screaming, "No, you are not."

We don't fight the spin with forced positivity. We fight it with a better question.

A precise, powerful question is a circuit breaker.

It forces the system to reboot and re-evaluate its priority list. It shifts your energy instantly from the chaotic world of Rumination to the grounded world of Practicality.

This is the basis of the Stoic Instant-Shift Prompts. They are simple. They are direct. They hijack the spiral.

1. WHAT IS THE SINGLE PRODUCTIVE ACTION AVAILABLE TO ME RIGHT NOW?

PANIC LOVES GRAND, OVERWHELMING SCHEMES. IT LOVES TO DWELL on the totality of the failure. It hates single, small steps.

When the noise starts demanding a five-year plan for career redemption or a complete overhaul of your personality, you stop it dead.

What is the next physical movement?

The next email?

The next phone call?

The next sip of water?

Focusing on the micro-action pulls your awareness out of the vast, terrifying future and grounds it in the present reality of effort. The brain cannot efficiently spiral and complete a task simultaneously. Choose the task.

2. IS THIS SOMETHING I CAN INFLUENCE, OR IS IT SOMETHING I MUST ACCEPT?

This is the Stoic Dichotomy of Control. It is the core hammer of peace.

If the answer is you cannot influence it—the actions of your neighbour, the decision of your former boss, the weather, the outcome of a financial market—then the energy drain stops. Immediately.

You are not required to hold anxiety over things you cannot affect. That anxiety is useless. It is chronic noise.

If you can influence it, great. See prompt number one. What is the productive action?

If you cannot influence it, you redirect the energy toward acceptance. Acceptance is not defeat. It is simply stating the current state of reality. "This is happening. I accept this current fact." You are now free to focus on the tiny sliver of reality that remains yours: your response.

3. WHAT ARE THE NEUTRAL, OBSERVABLE FACTS OF THIS SITUATION?

THE MALFUNCTIONING SMOKE ALARM DOES NOT REPORT FACTS. IT reports interpretations, predictions, and emotional projections.

It says, "You are a total failure."

That is not a fact.

You need to strip away the story and find the kernel of truth underneath.

Fact: I did not receive the promotion I wanted.

Fact: I said a harsh word to my spouse.

Fact: I have $400 less in my account than I anticipated.

Facts are calm. They are concrete. They are manageable. The story—"I am ruined," "My life is falling apart," "I am terrible at relationships"—is chaos.

Use this prompt to force your mind back down to the ground. Get granular. The smaller the fact, the less terrifying it is.

4. HOW CRITICAL IS THIS CRISIS IF I VIEW IT FROM 30 DAYS IN THE FUTURE?

WE SUFFER NOT FROM THE ACTUAL EVENT, BUT FROM THE JUDGMENT we attach to the event right now. The present moment is designed to feel maximal. Everything feels like a catastrophe.

We must apply the temporal check.

Take the current crisis and mentally fast-forward the clock one month. Or one year.

Will this argument matter?

Will this minor rejection matter?

Will this immediate financial concern matter, or will it simply be a data point in a much longer narrative?

Viewing the current moment from the future immediately shrinks the scale of the problem. It transforms a catastrophe into an incident. It transforms inevitable doom into a difficult Tuesday.

5. What is the true, inescapable downside, and can I survive it?

This is called premeditation of evils, or premeditation malorum.

Your brain is already panicking about the worst-case scenario. It's just doing it vaguely, which makes it worse. Vague fears are always heavier than precise ones.

We bring the worst case out into the light and define it.

If I quit my job, I lose my income and health benefits.

If I tell my friend the truth, they might be angry and leave.

Once you have the defined, worst-case scenario, you ask the second question: Can I survive that?

Yes. Almost always, the answer is yes. It will be hard, messy, painful, and inconvenient. But survival is certain.

Defining the downside and acknowledging your ability to survive it removes the fear of the unknown. And the unknown is the primary fuel source for panic.

Use these five questions like a spiritual wrench set. Keep them close. The second the volume spikes, pull out the appropriate prompt and force the brain to answer the question, not repeat the noise.

THE ABSURDITY DEFLATOR: HOW LIGHT-HEARTEDNESS AND LAUGHTER INSTANTLY CRIPPLE OVERWHELMING SERIOUSNESS

THE ANXIETY BRAIN IS A FUNDAMENTALLY SERIOUS BRAIN.

It takes itself too seriously.

It takes every potential disaster and elevates it.

It puts the disaster under a harsh spotlight.

It adds dramatic, terrible music.

The brain whispers: This is paramount. This defines you. This is an urgent, existential threat.

This seriousness is the fuel for the fire. If the anxiety is treated as deeply important and gravely meaningful, it gains power. It gains authority. It demands reverence.

Humor is the instant antidote.

It is the Absurdity Deflator.

It's the simplest, most powerful way to defuse a serious thought without getting stuck arguing with it.

You cannot simultaneously laugh deeply and feel existentially threatened by the content of a thought. The two cognitive states are neurologically incompatible. Laughter is a circuit breaker. It forces a cognitive defusion because it requires stepping back and observing the situation from a distance.

When the smoke alarm brain starts shrieking about a future disaster, it relies entirely on you treating that threat with deference. It needs you to lean in, listen intently, and panic.

We break the cycle with absurdity.

When you notice a catastrophic thought—I will fail this presentation and lose everything—don't try to counter it with a positive affirmation. That keeps the thought serious. It keeps you fighting on the thought's turf.

Instead, change the context.

Make it ridiculous.

One powerful technique is personification through farce.

We talked about naming the inner critic. Now, give that critic a ridiculous voice and a stupid hat.

Hear the thought: You are a disaster waiting to happen.

Now, rerun that audio track in the voice of a grumpy gnome who lives in your microwave. Or a pompous British butler with a squeaky voice.

You are going to fail and everyone will judge you, delivered by Elmer Fudd.

Immediately, the intensity collapses. The high-stakes threat—which requires a deep, sober internalization—collapses into a low-stakes joke.

Why does this work?

Because absurdity highlights the distance between you, the observer, and the inner noise, the performance.

The thought hasn't been solved. The fear hasn't vanished. But the power, the grip, is severed. The thought is exposed as silly theater, not sober reality.

Humor is a profound act of disrespect toward your internal tyrant.

When the mind demands you take the fear of future ruin seriously, laugh instead. It doesn't mean you are ignoring productive planning. It means you are refusing to be terrorized by the narrative.

If a serious thought repeats, exaggerate it to the point of impossibility.

My boss hates me.

No, your boss loves you so much they are going to commission a bronze statue of you for the lobby. They are going to name their firstborn child after you. They are going to declare a national holiday in your honor.

This is not lying to yourself. This is active defusion. You are using the cognitive mechanism of satire to break the hypnotic seriousness of the thought loop.

The malfunctioning smoke alarm depends on high alert. High seriousness. High vigilance. It needs you frozen and worried.

Laughter breaks the paralysis. It injects energy and perspective. It reminds you that even the worst potential outcome is something that happens, not something that defines you.

Use light-heartedness aggressively.

It is the single fastest way to pull yourself out of the gravitational field of an overblown worry. When everything feels overwhelming, ask yourself the most powerful question:

What is funny about this situation?

What is the most ridiculous, over-the-top exaggeration of this fear?

You are not fighting your thoughts. You are simply refusing to respect them. You are turning the drama into a puppet show.

Remember this: Seriousness demands your obedience. Absurdity grants you immediate freedom. Choose the rebellion.

—★–★–★—

THE LOW-STAKES MASTERY PLAN: HOW TO PROGRAM THE NEW CALM RESPONSE PATTERN THROUGH TINY, DAILY PRACTICE RUNS

We are not aiming for perfection.

Stop trying to launch yourself into a state of permanent, blinding inner peace through one heroic effort. It won't work. You'll crash and burn. You'll label yourself a failure.

Mastery is not a destination. It's a habit.

If you want to program the new, calmer operating system—the one where your inner narrator is objective, not panicked—you must train it in low-stakes environments.

We need practice runs. Tiny, zero-consequence repetitions that build neural pathways without triggering the full-scale trauma response.

You cannot learn to defuse an intrusive thought during a panic attack if you haven't practiced it while waiting for the kettle to boil.

The stakes must be low. Your environment must be safe.

Here are the low-stakes practice runs that log the necessary repetition. Do one or two every day.

The Four-Second Traffic Jam

Every time you are stuck at a red light or in slow-moving traffic, that is your training moment.

Traffic is universal annoyance. It triggers that low-grade frustration. It activates the Planner persona: "This is inefficient. I am wasting time. I should have left earlier."

Instead of merging with that frustration, practice the objective observer role.

This is simple.

Just state, internally: “I am stopped. I am safe. I am having the feeling of annoyance.”

Do not pull out the phone. Do not start reviewing your calendar.

Just notice the physical tension that traffic generates in your shoulders or jaw.

Then, deliberately release that tension. Even if it’s just for four seconds.

This practice run teaches your brain that a minor inconvenience is not a catastrophe. It teaches your body how to relax in a stressful situation that you cannot control.

You are logging a rep for Radical Acceptance.

The Line-Up Defusion

When you are waiting in line—at the grocery store, at the bank, for the elevator—the mind hates it.

Waiting feels non-productive. The Boredom Trigger starts searching for problems to solve. It starts rehearsing arguments or criticizing the person in front of you.

This is your opportunity to practice thought defusion.

Instead of believing the criticism, step back.

Listen to the committee argue. Give them a mental wave.

"Hello, Critic. I see you want to judge that person's shoes. Noted."

Then, deliberately focus on a sensory detail of the immediate environment. The smell of the coffee shop. The sound of the music. The weight of your feet on the floor.

You are practicing pulling back from the map (the internal narrative) and grounding in the territory (the reality of the present moment).

Every time you wait in line and choose to observe your thoughts instead of following them, you strengthen the neutral narrator.

The Typo Protocol

Your inner critic lives for mistakes.

You sent an email with a typo. You dropped a glass. You forgot one item on the grocery list.

In the past, this minor slip would trigger a chain reaction of self-flagellation: "I always mess up. I am so careless. I can't handle anything."

This is a high-yield training moment.

The instant the mistake is made and the Critic screams, you must interrupt the pattern.

Use the absurd reality check.

Did dropping the glass end your career? No. Did the typo collapse the global economy? No.

The goal here is not to feel positive about the mistake. The goal is neutrality.

Practice this sentence, firmly: "A mistake occurred. This does not define my competence."

Then, immediately move to action: clean up the glass, send the correction, make a note for tomorrow.

This exercise is training your brain to decouple error from identity. It teaches that the objective solution is the priority, not the emotional spiral of shame.

Logging the Reps, Not Seeking the Rush

This plan works because it is dull.

It lacks the drama of a major confrontation. It lacks the profound revelation of an eight-day silent retreat.

It's just tiny actions. Repeated.

Each time you choose the new calm response in a low-stakes moment, you are literally reinforcing a new neural circuit. You are making the old path of anxiety fainter. You are making the new path of objective observation stronger.

Mastery is built through this kind of consistency. It is the cumulative power of a thousand micro-choices that you make during boring, normal moments.

Don't wait for the crisis to prove you are calm. Prove it now, when nothing is happening.

The greatest breakthroughs in peace often come not during meditation, but when you simply observe your thoughts about traffic and choose to relax your jaw.

It's small. It's quiet. It is how the new code becomes default.

CHAPTER EIGHT

Personality Protected: How Achieving Peace Makes You More Interesting, Not Boring

LET'S TALK ABOUT THE BIGGEST LIE YOU BELIEVE RIGHT NOW.

It's the silent fear deep in your gut.

It's the one that whispers: If I stop worrying, if I stop feeling this intense dread, I will become boring.

I will become a beige human being.

You think your anxiety is your edge. You think your constant analysis, your obsessive planning, your hyper-vigilance—you think that's what makes you smart. Or passionate. Or interesting.

You look at truly calm people and you think they must be detached. You think they must be secretly dull. You assume they have sacrificed their fire to find their peace.

Stop it right there.

This is the central myth that keeps brilliant, driven people locked in cycles of chaos. They mistake reactivity for reality. They mistake drama for depth.

Your anxiety is not your personality. It is the cage that holds your personality hostage.

It's the static on the line. It drowns out your actual voice.

We are not aiming for the life of a 'chill robot.' I promise you that. We are aiming for a life where your best traits—your wit, your empathy, your sharp intelligence, your unique sense of humor—finally have the space to breathe and express themselves without the constant interference of fear.

The truth is simple. Peace doesn't suppress you. It amplifies you.

Think about the times you felt truly magnetic. Was it when you were panicked, rambling, or rehearsing? No. It was when you were present. It was when you were listening intently. It was when you delivered a joke that landed perfectly because your timing wasn't rushed by internal noise.

Your energy is already massive. Your drive is already potent. The only difference is that right now, 90 percent of that magnificent energy is being used internally. It's fighting fires that don't exist. It's running diagnostics on systems that are fine. It is fuel pouring out of a hole in the tank.

When you achieve psychological peace, you don't lose the fuel. You patch the tank.

Now, all that inherent, vibrant energy is suddenly available for creation. For love. For deep work. For meaningful play.

You become more interesting because you are no longer performing.

Performance is exhausting. Trying to convince others (and yourself) that you are okay, smart, or successful despite the internal screaming is a full-time job.

When you drop the mask of the chaotic, hyper-alert person, you are left with the authentic self. And the authentic self is almost always far more fascinating than the anxious, trying-too-hard defense mechanism.

The chaos is predictable. The anxious pattern is repetitive. The peace is the foundation for true originality.

The energy you thought you needed for worrying is the energy you now use for living.

THE MYTH OF THE CHILL ROBOT

Let's dismantle the idea that true passion requires mental instability.

Some of the most high-performing, passionate people on earth are exceptionally calm. They aren't low-energy. They are highly efficient energy users.

Look at a brilliant athlete. When do they perform their best? In the eye of the storm. When they are totally present. When their thoughts are quiet. Their body moves with passion, but their mind is still. If they were controlled by the anxious committee—What if I fail? What if I miss this shot? What will they think?—they would freeze. They would miss.

Passion is deep engagement with the present task.

Anxiety is deep engagement with a feared future or a shamed past.

Peace is the necessary prerequisite for maximum human performance.

Think about your creative outlets, whatever they are. Writing. Music. Cooking. Planning a huge project. When does the real insight hit? It hits when you step away. When you stop forcing it. When the pressure is released and your brain finally has room to connect disparate ideas.

This space, this mental stillness, is the ultimate competitive edge.

The anxious brain sees a problem and immediately starts to panic and search for a hundred solutions simultaneously. It scatters effort.

The calm brain sees the problem, takes a breath, categorizes it (Chapter 4), and directs laser-like focus toward the most leveraged action.

The anxious person seems passionate but burns out quickly. They are driven by avoidance.

The peaceful person seems stable but has reserves of energy that last for years. They are driven by purpose.

Which one is truly more powerful? Which one is truly more captivating?

A person who can hold a large, complex vision without panicking is captivating. A person who can process setbacks without dissolving into self-pity is captivating. A person whose inner life is structured and stable is a magnet for opportunity and connection.

THE LIE OF SELF-ERASURE

We must be very clear about this: The methods in this book—thought defusion, neutralizing the critic, establishing boundaries of control—are not about removing parts of yourself.

They are about removing the parts that aren't you.

Your messy, brilliant, flawed, wonderful identity is what we are protecting.

Self-help often pushes the idea that you must become "less." Less sensitive. Less angry. Less emotional. Less you. It demands self-erasure.

This is a disastrous strategy. Trying to cut off a part of your personality because it sometimes causes you pain is like amputating a finger because it once got jammed in a door.

Your sensitivity is not the problem. The reaction to your sensitivity—the rumination, the self-criticism, the anxiety spirals—that is the problem.

When you apply the Code, your sensitivity remains. It just turns into empathy instead of panic.

Your intensity remains. It just turns into focus instead of frenzy.

Your dark humor remains. It just becomes funnier because it's not laced with genuine, urgent self-loathing.

We are accepting your whole messy self. We are just stopping the internal civil war.

When the internal civil war stops, you are finally freed up to be radically, authentically who you are. The energy that was defending your identity can now be used to express it.

That is the definition of interesting.

THE RIPPLE EFFECT

INTERNAL STABILITY DOESN'T JUST BENEFIT YOU. IT REVOLUTIONIZES your relationships.

When you are internally quiet, you become a better friend. A better partner. A better colleague.

Why? Because you become truly present.

Think about what happens when you try to listen to someone while your internal committee is screaming:

Are they judging me right now? I should interrupt with my clever anecdote. I need to figure out what I'm going to say next. I hope they don't ask about that mistake I made last week.

You are not listening. You are waiting to talk. You are constantly triaging your own mental state.

When you practice defusion and grounding, the noise drops. You are just there. Open. Unflustered.

When you interact with people from a place of genuine peace, you offer them something rare and powerful: a safe space.

Your stability acts as an emotional anchor for the people you care about. When a crisis hits your partnership, the person with the loud brain amplifies the chaos. The person with the quiet brain contains the chaos. They become the resource. The solid ground.

People are not drawn to drama. They are drawn to reliability and presence.

Your emotional regulation revolutionizes communication. You stop reacting defensively to perceived slights because you no longer believe every thought that whispers about being attacked. You can hear the actual content of the conversation. You stop projecting your fear onto others.

You become a rock star collaborator. A thoughtful lover. A non-reactive parent.

This is not boring. This is a profound, life-altering power.

The Synthesis: Feeling Deeply Without Being Swept Away

The final point we must synthesize is this balance: feeling deeply, yet maintaining stability.

Some people worry that psychological work is about numbing yourself to pain. That's toxic suppression (which we covered in Chapter 5). We reject that entirely.

We want you to feel the full spectrum of human experience.

We want you to feel the deep, heart-breaking beauty of life.

We want you to feel the thrilling joy of success.

We want you to feel the sting of disappointment.

The difference is how those feelings move through you.

The chaotic brain (fusion) is the feeling. You are swept away. The feeling takes over your judgment, dictates your narrative, and pulls you into rumination spirals for days. You are a ship lost in a storm.

The calm brain (defusion) observes the feeling. The feeling is a wave. You feel the full force of the water, but you remain standing on the shore, watching it crash, knowing it will recede.

You feel deeply. You cry the tears. You laugh the hard, joyful laugh. You mourn the loss.

But you do not identify your whole self with the temporary state.

The pain hurts, but it doesn't define you.

The joy thrills you, but it doesn't make you overconfident and reckless.

This synthesis—deep engagement coupled with radical stability—is what makes people truly alive.

It is the opposite of boring. It is the definition of maturity and wisdom.

Your personality is not only protected. It is finally liberated.

You have cleared the noise so your own brilliant signal can broadcast clearly, powerfully, and consistently.

Go be interesting. Go be passionately stable. The world needs the real, quieted you, not the frantic performer you used to be.

THE MYTH OF THE CHILL ROBOT: WHY TRUE PASSION REQUIRES MENTAL STABILITY (AND HOW PEACE AMPLIFIES YOUR COMPETITIVE EDGE)

YOU FEAR BECOMING BLAND.

You worry that if you stop overthinking, you stop caring. You believe the noise in your head is proof of how much effort you are putting in.

If the chaos goes quiet, doesn't the passion die?

This is the Myth of the Chill Robot. It's the idea that managing your anxiety means becoming an unfeeling, passive automaton. That you trade your brilliance and intensity for a flatline of mild contentment.

We need to kill this myth now.

The opposite is true.

Passion is not the same as frenzy.

Frenzy is scattered fire. It is nervous energy. It feels productive because it's fast and exhausting. But it lacks direction. It burns out quickly and leaves you with smoke inhalation.

True passion is focused heat. It is a controlled burn.

Think of the person who accomplishes something truly difficult. The creator. The builder. The strategic thinker. Were they driven by panic? No. They were driven by clarity.

Passion requires tremendous mental space.

It requires the ability to hold a complex idea without immediately panicking over its feasibility.

You need stability to sustain high-level performance.

Your brain can only produce two things at full capacity: anxiety management, or focused execution. It cannot do both simultaneously and sustainably.

When you are stressed, half of your operating system is dedicated to managing the internal threat assessment. The screaming committee is exhausting resources. You are constantly debating, negotiating, and defending yourself against your own mind.

How much energy does that leave for your actual goal? Maybe fifty percent. Maybe less.

Now, imagine the internal argument is gone.

Imagine the critic has been defused. The paranoia has been categorized and released. The energy that was previously used to wrestle yourself to the floor is now available.

This is why peace is the ultimate competitive edge.

The peace we are building here is not passive surrender. It is aggressive energy conservation.

While your competitors are spending 70% of their bandwidth dealing with emotional friction, you are channelling 100% into the work.

You are seeing the field clearly.

You are making decisions based on objective reality, not fear.

The high-performance athlete isn't the one running around screaming before the race. It's the one standing still. The one whose mind is silent, processing exactly what needs to be done.

That stillness is the amplifier.

When you remove the noise, you don't remove the signal. You remove the static.

The core of who you are—your drive, your creativity, your intense desire to win—that signal gets louder. It becomes undeniable.

A calm mind does not kill ambition. It sharpens it.

It turns vague, anxious ambition into laser-focused, executable intent.

You do not lose your fire when you find peace. You simply install the container that allows that fire to burn hotter, longer, and more powerfully than you ever thought possible.

You stop being driven by fear of failure and start being driven by genuine desire. That difference is everything. That is the secret to enduring passion.

THE LIE OF SELF-ERASURE: WHY YOU MUST NEVER DISCARD YOUR MESSY, BRILLIANT IDENTITY TO FIND LASTING CALM

We must talk about the biggest, most damaging lie in modern self-help.

The lie is this: To find peace, you must find a version of yourself that is less.

Less intense. Less opinionated. Less messy. Less sensitive.

The myth of spiritual enlightenment often translates into the demand for self-erasure.

You are encouraged to discard your sharp edges. To sand down your strong personality. To eliminate the high energy that makes you, frankly, fascinating.

This culture tells you that calm is equivalent to neutrality. That true peace means being perfectly pliable and void of conflict.

That is a promise of psychological flatness.

It is a promise of becoming generic.

And it fails because your "messy, brilliant identity" is the core engine of your life.

The traits you are told to discard—the intensity, the obsessive drive, the deep empathy that sometimes leads to pain—these are also the components of your success and your uniqueness.

If you succeed in carving them out, you don't achieve peace.

You achieve depletion.

You achieve a kind of psychological exhaustion from trying to maintain a blank slate identity that was never meant to be.

We came here for a very different outcome.

We are not trying to create a chill robot.

We are not aiming for a void where your personality used to live.

The entire premise of this book is protection, not destruction.

We are learning to turn the volume down on the noise so that your true signal—the brilliant, complex, driven self—can finally get through.

We are not silencing the critical voice by eliminating your drive. We are simply recognizing that the voice is a flawed software program.

We keep the hard drive. We keep the data. We keep the genius.

Peace is not the opposite of passion.

Peace is the necessary foundation for sustained, effective passion.

When the noise is managed, your identity doesn't disappear. It amplifies.

The energy you spent worrying about being too much, or too loud, or too complicated, is suddenly released back into the world—directed and clean.

You are allowed to be deeply ambitious and calmly centered.

You are allowed to be highly sensitive and internally stable.

You are allowed to keep your sharp edges, your dark sense of humor, and your tendency to obsess over things you love.

We simply made sure that obsession serves you, instead of enslaving you.

Never let a self-help guru convince you that you must erase the best parts of yourself to find relief.

Your identity is not the problem.

The problem was the broken operating system running your identity.

We fixed the code.

Now go be exactly who you are. All of it. Messy and brilliant.

THE RIPPLE EFFECT: THE UNEXPECTED WAY YOUR INTERNAL STABILITY REVOLUTIONIZES YOUR FRIENDSHIPS AND PARTNERSHIPS

You thought this journey was private.

Just you and your internal noise.

That's the lie the messy brain tells you.

Internal stability is never a solitary act.

It is a shockwave.

It moves outward immediately.

It hits every person you interact with. Every day.

It fundamentally changes the atmosphere of your home.

You become something different for them. You become reliable.

Think about the most common arguments in your life.

What fuels them?

It's usually two loud brains crashing together. Two smoke alarms shrieking at the same time.

Two egos fighting for air and validation.

When your smoke alarm is quiet, you stop taking everything personally.

You don't panic when your partner raises their voice. You don't internalize your colleague's bad mood as a personal failing.

Because your value is no longer tied to their momentary instability.

You can hear the actual words. Not just the perceived threat implied by your fear.

You create space.

That space is the deepest gift you can give a relationship. That space is where true connection can breathe.

Now consider the opposite: your attention.

How often do you listen to a friend while you are rehearsing your own response?

Or while you are frantically solving your own internal problems?

You are half-here. That is disrespectful.

A quiet mind listens fully. It is present.

That is the greatest gift you can give anyone. Pure, unadulterated presence.

When you are stable, your colleague tells you about a project and you hear the details. You don't filter those details through your own insecurity first.

Your friend tells you about their deep pain. You are a steady, unmoving pole in their storm. Not a shaky reflection of their drama.

This stability reduces the immense emotional labor required of others.

When you learn to soothe yourself—through the tools in this book—you stop outsourcing that job.

You stop demanding that your partner fill the void.

This is revolutionary for a long-term partnership.

They are no longer your full-time therapist. They are not required to constantly regulate your mood because you can't.

They can just be your partner. They can just be your friend.

That removes the suffocating pressure of dependency. It gives them back their emotional freedom.

And that freedom is what makes them want to stay, happily.

At work, stability is not just helpful. It is a superpower.

You become the indispensable one.

You are the person who stays centered when chaos hits the office. When the deadline shifts or the budget collapses.

You are making decisions based on facts. Not on fear.

The ability to pause before replying—the skill of non-fusion—is worth a massive raise.

It's perceived as immediate competence.

People trust the calm voice. They want to follow the person who isn't running on panic fuel.

Your internal peace simplifies everything for those around you. It creates a safe harbor.

The best, most generous thing you can do for the people you love is learn to manage yourself.

It is not selfish to pursue a quiet mind. It is the deepest form of generosity.

You are giving them the gift of a stable, consistent atmosphere.

You are giving them the gift of yourself, unfiltered, and truly present for the first time.

That ripple changes everything.

THE SYNTHESIS: THE SECRET TO FEELING DEEPLY WITHOUT BEING SWEPT AWAY BY YOUR FEELINGS

This is the most critical distinction we will ever make.

It's the fear that keeps people clinging to their anxiety.

The fear is this: If I stop worrying, if I get truly calm, I'll stop caring. I'll become bland. I'll lose my edge. I will be boring.

You think your anxiety is the source of your passion. You think the noise fuels your drive.

It doesn't. It drains it.

The synthesis is the point where you get to experience the sheer, overwhelming intensity of life without being knocked down by it.

It's about volume, not silence.

We aren't trying to mute the experience. We are trying to turn down the internal static. The background hum of the committee.

When the static goes away, the music of your actual emotional life gets louder. And clearer.

Stability doesn't make you numb. It grants you capacity.

Imagine your consciousness is a glass.

If that glass is already half-full of worry, rumination, and stress (the noise), when a powerful feeling arrives—a true passion, a deep sorrow, a magnificent joy—the glass overflows instantly.

You are swept away. You lose control. You become reactive. You merge with the emotion because there is no space left for observation.

The work of the Calm Mind Code is not about draining the glass of feelings. It's about making the glass bigger.

It's removing the chronic noise so that when the real, massive, profound feelings come, you have the architecture to contain them.

You can feel everything.

You can feel the searing intensity of a breakthrough idea. You can feel the sharp, deep pang of grief when you lose something important. You can feel the electric surge of love.

And you can feel it deeply—down to your bones—without losing your footing.

This is the secret to feeling deeply without being swept away. It's the constant presence of the Objective Observer we spent Chapter 7 training.

When true pain hits, the observer doesn't try to fix it. It doesn't scream, "This is intolerable!"

The observer says: "Hello, grief. You are powerful. You are present. You are not me, but you are inside me right now."

That small separation—that simple act of naming and accepting—is the lever that prevents the flood.

You get to experience the full human spectrum of emotion. You get to be fully alive. But you retain the stability of the shore.

When you are fused with your emotions, they are a flood that washes away your decisions.

When you are synthesized—stable yet feeling—they are raw data. They inform you. They color your life. They provide the depth and texture that defines your soul. But they don't dictate your behavior.

This is why calm people are often the most passionate.

They have the mental bandwidth to dedicate their energy to the pursuit of joy or excellence. They aren't constantly bleeding energy fighting internal ghosts.

Their internal stability acts as an amplifier.

When they feel joy, it isn't diluted by a background worry about how long the joy will last. It is pure.

When they feel anger, it is quickly processed, not allowed to spiral into destructive rumination. It becomes fuel for constructive action.

The goal was never detachment. It was capacity.

The goal was always maximum experience, grounded in minimum internal chaos.

You do not lose your passion. You refine it.

You swap out the jittery, anxious, frantic energy of the malfunctioning smoke alarm brain for the deep, consistent power of a reactor core.

It's reliable. It's clean. And it allows you to finally stand firm in the deepest waters of your own soul. You can feel everything now. Go feel it.

CHAPTER NINE

The Code Applied: Integrating the Calm Mind System for Permanent, Sustainable Peace

YOU MADE IT.

We walked through the noise together.

You have the manual now. You built the code. You understand the mechanics of your messy, magnificent brain.

This is the chapter about the long game. This is about integration.

Because here is the critical, unromantic truth: The work is never done.

It never stops.

You don't get a certificate of permanent calm. You don't reach the summit and then retire the hiking boots.

You acquire a maintenance contract.

You transition from a state of crisis management to a state of continuous, gentle maintenance. That is what sustainable peace looks like. It is not the absence of storms. It is the ability to navigate them without sinking your own boat.

So how do we apply this code permanently? How do we weave Defusion and Control and Neutrality into the fabric of a noisy Tuesday afternoon?

We start small.

We stop demanding radical overhaul. We focus on micro-decisions.

The most powerful psychological changes are always incremental. They are boring. They are reliable.

You do not need a three-hour retreat. You need three seconds of awareness right now.

THE FIRST THREE SECONDS

The entire Calm Mind System hinges on recognizing the split-second gap between a stimulus and your reaction.

That is where your power lives.

The difficult email lands. The dog barks at 3 AM. A colleague makes a passive-aggressive comment.

Stimulus.

Before this book, the sequence was automatic: Stimulus, Fusion, Emotion, Reaction, Regret.

The Code Application is simple: We insert a space.

We insert the Observer (Chapter 7). We deploy Defusion (Chapter 2). We check the Control categories (Chapter 4).

Integration means automating this pause.

The trigger happens. The Committee starts screaming its usual script.

Your job now is not to shut the Committee up. Your job is simply to notice it started talking.

That's Defusion.

It is saying: "This is a catastrophe. You always mess this up."

You respond—internally, neutrally—with: "Ah. I am having the thought that this is a catastrophe."

See the difference?

You didn't fight the thought. You didn't argue with it. You didn't even challenge its premise.

You just labeled it. You placed it in the "Thought" column. You stripped it of its authority.

This is the most critical habit for sustainability. You stop arguing with the weather inside your head. You just note that it is raining.

MAINTENANCE IS THE NEW PERFECTION

We must abandon the expectation of perfection immediately.

If you believe that mastery means never getting angry, or never worrying, or never having an intrusive thought again, you have missed the point entirely.

That is the spiritual lie we rejected in the Introduction.

Your brain is a problem-solving machine. It will continue to find problems until the day you die. That is its function.

The goal is not to break the machine. The goal is to install better software for when it inevitably runs a bug.

True integration looks messy.

It looks like having a terrible argument, but remembering five minutes later to perform the Somatic Discharge (Chapter 5) instead of brooding for five hours.

It looks like falling into a shame spiral for twenty minutes, but realizing: "Wait. I am fused. This is the Rehearsing Shame loop." And then using the Instant-Shift Prompt (Chapter 7): "What can I do right now?"

The metric for success is not the presence of peace. It is the duration of the noise.

How quickly can you pull yourself out?

That speed is your power. That speed is your integration score.

The person who can snap back from a catastrophic thought in 30 seconds is exponentially more peaceful than the person who avoids catastrophic thoughts 95% of the time, only to be crippled by the 5% that remain.

You are training for resilience, not immunity.

THE SHIFT TO LOW-STAKES PRACTICE

We often wait for massive, life-altering events to test our mental tools.

The job loss. The breakup. The severe illness.

That's like waiting for the championship game to try a new move. Too much pressure. Too high a stake.

Sustainable integration requires practicing the code during the low-stakes moments. This trains the muscle memory.

Think about the everyday annoyances. These are your training drills.

You are stuck in traffic. Traffic is uncontrollable (Chapter 4).

Old Code: Fury. Honking. Rumination about why you left late. The Worry Tax (Chapter 3).

New Code: Defusion applied instantly. "I am having the thought that traffic should move faster. That is the Futility Trap."

Action: Breathe. Focus on the high-leverage area: Maybe listen to the audio course you've been putting off. Accept the reality.

Your child spills an entire bowl of cereal. You are tired.

Old Code: Yelling. Inner Critic screaming, "You're a terrible parent who can't even handle cereal."

New Code: The Micro-Pause (Chapter 5). A physical step back. Precision labeling: "I feel frustration. My body feels tight. This is somatic tension." Discharge: Shake out the hands for ten seconds.

Then: Narrator Shift (Chapter 7). "Cereal spilled. It is a moment of chaos. Not a judgment of my worth."

These tiny interactions—the spilled coffee, the slow internet, the minor disagreement—these are the arenas where you program the new default.

You don't need to be perfect when your world is falling apart. You need to be programmed when the world is merely annoying.

THE CALM MIND CODE AS A FILTER

When you fully integrate the Code, it stops feeling like a separate action and starts feeling like a filter through which you view reality.

It is your new OS.

It simplifies decision-making.

Every piece of information, every worry, every interaction, gets automatically run through two filters:

Filter 1: Is this thought fact or fiction? (Defusion)

Filter 2: Is this within my sphere of influence? (Control)

If the answer to Filter 1 is "Fiction" (it's a projection, a fear, a judgment) and the answer to Filter 2 is "No," the material is instantly discarded. No energy spent.

Imagine the sheer volume of mental bandwidth this frees up.

Ninety percent of the noise in your brain—the constant, screaming committee—exists in the intersection of Fear and Lack of Control.

When you filter those inputs out, you are left with the 10% that requires practical attention.

This is the power of neutrality. You are not trying to be happy about the mess. You are simply refusing to spend your finite energy budget on materials you cannot use.

That is sustainable energy conservation. That is the 10x ROI (Chapter 4).

THE REALIZATION OF UNCOVERING PEACE

For the longest time, you probably believed that peace was something you had to achieve.

A place you had to reach. A spiritual medal you had to earn.

That belief is exhausting. It forces you to chase and strive and hustle for something that is already yours.

The ultimate integration point of the Calm Mind System is the realization that peace is not acquired. It is uncovered.

It is your default setting.

Think of it like this: If you took a beautiful, antique wooden table and threw fifty cans of paint on it—layers of worry, fear, fusion, anxiety, and self-criticism—you wouldn't need to build a new table.

You would need to strip away the paint.

The table is the core self. The peace. The underlying sanity. It is strong, stable, and already there.

The Code is the stripping agent.

It dissolves the paint of fusion. It sands away the old scripts of the critic. It cleans up the mess of the uncontrollable.

You are not creating calm. You are revealing it.

And because it is your native state, it requires less energy to maintain than the noise does. The noise requires constant attention, fuel, and belief. Calm requires nothing but the absence of interference.

This realization flips the entire process. You stop chasing. You start allowing.

You allow the thoughts to be thoughts. You allow the feelings to be feelings. You allow the world to be the chaotic, uncontrollable place that it is.

And in that allowing, in that gentle release of the steering wheel, you find stillness.

The integration is simply choosing, in every micro-moment, to stop interfering with your own default peace.

It is a discipline of non-effort.

Keep the code close. Use it often. Get messy. Fail fast. Snap back quicker.

This is your life, now running on the Calm Mind System.

——★–★–★——

THE TINY HABITS RULE: IMPLEMENTING INCREMENTAL CHANGES THAT GUARANTEE LONG-TERM SUCCESS WITHOUT OVERHAULING YOUR LIFE

YOU TRIED THE HUGE GOAL, DIDN'T YOU?

We all have.

The grand overhaul. The massive life change. The sudden decision to become a perfect, spiritually awakened person overnight.

How did that work out?

It failed. They always fail. They are built on motivation. Motivation is a fleeting, unreliable drug. It lasts for three days, maybe a week, and then the chaos of real life shows up and blows your perfect plan to dust.

We are done with heroic efforts.

We are implementing the Tiny Habits Rule.

This is the anti-perfection plan. This is how the Calm Mind Code becomes a permanent fixture in your operating system without you noticing the effort.

The rule is this: If you want consistency, you must aim for actions that are too small to fail.

Too small to even require motivation.

If your goal is to build muscle, you don't start by scheduling a two-hour workout. You start by doing one push-up. One. That's it. You can skip the rest of the workout, but you cannot skip that one push-up.

It's about creating a momentum so gentle that inertia doesn't even notice you moving.

When we apply this to the mind, we are looking for micro-interventions. Moments of defusion or grounding that take four seconds or less.

You are not blocking out fifteen minutes to sit and process your trauma. That is intense. That is unsustainable.

You are hijacking the small, existing routines of your day to anchor the new behavior.

This is called habit stacking.

Let's look at the Code applied incrementally.

The moment you sit down in your office chair: That is your trigger.

The action is not to reflect on your day. The action is to name three colors you can see. Red, gray, blue. That's it. You are grounded. You just pulled your mind out of the future and into the present. Four seconds.

The moment you take the first sip of coffee: That is your trigger.

The action is to silently observe the taste, the heat, and the weight of the mug. That is a full body-scan. That is micro-mindfulness. Four seconds.

The moment you catch the Inner Critic screaming an old script: That is your trigger.

The action is to use the Absurdity Deflator. You don't argue with the thought. You say, in your head, "Hello, Paranoid Planner, thanks for the warning," and immediately turn your attention back to the task at hand.

One sentence. One breath. That is the new response pattern.

The goal here is volume of repetition, not intensity of effort.

Your brain doesn't care if your actions are dramatic. It only cares about frequency. Every time you successfully execute a four-second defusion, you reinforce the neural pathway for calm. You tell the system: This is the new default.

We are not aiming for 100% success on one massive goal. We are aiming for 90% consistency on ten tiny habits.

If you miss the giant goal, you feel shame. You stop trying.

If you miss naming three colors once, it doesn't matter. It's too small to generate shame. You just do it the next time you sit down.

The Tiny Habits Rule makes failure almost irrelevant.

When you practice the Control Illusion categorization—separating the controllable from the uncontrollable—you don't do it for an hour of journaling. You do it when you open your email.

You scan the subject lines. Can I control the content of this email? No. I can only control my response.

One tiny clarity scan. Done.

The key to long-term sustainable peace is that your efforts must be invisible to your motivation system. They must be less effort than skipping them.

Try this today.

Identify one routine you already do without thinking—turning the key in the ignition, washing your hands, closing your laptop.

Attach one four-second Code action to it.

When the water hits my hands, I will immediately notice the temperature.

That's all you have to do.

You are planting quiet seeds of stability throughout your day. You are programming the calm mind system in the background, like a silent software update.

You don't need to quit your job. You don’t need to move to a cabin. You don't need a massive spiritual experience.

You just need to consistently and repeatedly choose the four-second response over the four-hour rumination.

That is how the Code moves from theory to instinct. Incrementally. Quietly. Permanently.

THE SETBACK PROTOCOL: YOUR QUICK-REFERENCE GUIDE FOR INSTANT THOUGHT DEFUSION WHEN RELAPSE HITS

IT WILL HAPPEN.

I need you to hear that clearly.

You will have a perfect week.

Maybe two.

You will feel the quiet. You will trust the calm. You will look around and think, “I finally solved it.”

Then Tuesday will hit.

A trigger pops up. A bad email lands. Someone cuts you off in traffic.

And suddenly, the smoke alarm is shrieking. The volume is at 100.

You will fall back into an old thought loop. You will feel that familiar shame: I failed. The code didn’t work. I am back to square one.

This is the most critical moment of your journey.

Because a relapse is not a failure. It is simply a temporary return to an old habit. It means your brain, which defaults to anxiety, found a familiar, well-worn path and decided to take a short, terrible vacation there.

Your mission is not to stop the vacation entirely.

Your mission is to shorten it.

We are aiming for speed of recovery, not perfection of practice.

The difference between successful long-term peace and chronic struggle is not how often you get tripped up. It is how fast you stand back up.

When the noise comes back, and it will, use this protocol. It is designed to be instantly deployable.

This is your Quick-Reference Guide.

THE SETBACK PROTOCOL: 3-STEP INSTANT DEFUSION

STEP 1: THE RECOGNITION AND NAMING PHASE

Your brain needs to stop fusing with the thought immediately. You need to create distance.

Stop everything.

Pull the hand brake. Literally pause whatever you are doing.

Identify the type of noise. Is this The Critic coming back? Is it The Paranoid Planner rehearsing disaster?

Name it out loud, or internally with force: "Oh, look. It's the Planner again."

Do not engage the content of the thought. Do not try to solve the noise.

Just label the noise.

The label is the sword. It cuts the fusion cord instantly.

Use the phrase: "I am having the thought that I am a failure."

Do not say: "I am a failure."

Recognition: I am in an old loop.

Naming: This is a forecasting loop.

STEP 2: SENSORY GROUNDING—THE 4-SECOND REALITY CHECK

When you relapse, your mental map just became the territory. You are lost in the theoretical future or the shameful past.

You need to anchor back to the physical, undeniable present. Right now.

The present moment is the only place the thought cannot live.

Focus entirely on the physical body for four seconds.

Where are your feet? Push them into the ground. Feel the texture of your shoes.

Where is your breath? Take one, slow, deliberate inhale. Feel the air hitting your upper lip on the exhale.

What can you see? Name three objects that are brown. Three objects that are rectangular.

Force your cognition away from abstraction and toward sensory facts.

This shifts the brain from the limbic system (panic) back into the frontal cortex (logic and awareness).

The noise cannot stand against hard, present-day facts.

Step 3: The Re-Entry Statement and Forgiveness

This is where you correct the emotional narrative of failure.

Do not allow the mistake to compound the suffering. You already made the mistake (the relapse). Don't make a second one (the self-flagellation).

Be objective. Be kind.

You simply returned to the default setting. It is not personal. It is neurological.

State your Re-Entry Command, firmly:

"I returned to the noise, but I am back now."

"This is a practice moment, not a failure."

"I do not require perfection, only consistency."

Then, gently, ask yourself: What is the very next, tiny, useful action I can take?

Not the perfect action. Not the complete solution.

Just the tiny, useful step.

Take that step. Even if it's just walking to the window and looking at the sky.

The noise is managed not by wrestling it into submission, but by simply out-manoeuvring it and walking away.

The key to the Setback Protocol is speed. The moment you realize you are drowning in noise, use Step 1 immediately. Do not wait for the wave to pass. Start labelling. Start feeling your feet.

Setbacks teach us where the foundation is weak. They are simply feedback.

Thank the noise for the lesson.

Then turn the volume down and get back to living.

THE LONG GAME: WHY MASTERY IS CONTINUOUS MAINTENANCE, NOT A ONE-TIME ACHIEVEMENT (AND HOW TO STOP EXPECTING PERFECTION)

You've done the work.

You have the manual now. You've practiced the defusion. You can name the critic. You know where the line is between planning and panic.

This is where the real truth lands.

There is no finish line.

You never graduate from this.

We need to address the deep-seated cultural lie that mastery is a one-time achievement. We love the narrative of the hero who learns the skill, defeats the villain, and rides off into permanent, peaceful sunshine.

That's a movie plot. It's not human psychology.

Your brain is a living, adapting organ. It's highly sensitive to stimuli, stress, caffeine, sugar, and the jerk in the car next to you. It is a machine designed by evolution to find problems. It will never stop performing its primary function, which is scanning the horizon for things that might kill you.

The Code you learned is not a permanent solution to turn off the machine.

It is a permanent maintenance schedule for the machine.

Think of it like dental hygiene. You don't brush your teeth perfectly once and say, "Great, my teeth are fixed forever." You brush them twice a day, every day, because the environment is constantly working to break them down.

Mental peace is the same continuous maintenance.

You are going to wake up tomorrow and your internal committee will be screaming again. They will be louder if you are tired. They will be vicious if you are stressed about money. They will be utterly convinced they are right if you just had a fight with your spouse.

Mastery is not defined by the absence of the committee.

It is defined by the speed with which you refuse to give them authority.

You are playing the long game. The long game is measured in moments of recovery, not years of stillness.

You might get swept away in a spiral. You might spend two hours ruminating over a professional slight. Before this book, that spiral might have lasted two weeks and cost you real sleep. Now, it lasts two hours.

That reduction in time? That is mastery.

Mastery is reducing the recovery time.

It is the ability to catch yourself earlier. To interrupt the script one sentence sooner. To deploy a grounding hack 30 minutes before the panic grips you.

Stop expecting perfection. Perfection is a fantasy created to make you feel inadequate. It is the ultimate quitting mechanism. If you expect zero noisy thoughts, you will fail every day, and eventually, you will throw the book across the room and say, "This doesn't work for me."

But it does work for you. You just needed to adjust the metric.

The metric is consistency, not flawlessness.

You don't have to be a spiritual guru radiating serenity. You just have to be a person who recognizes the smoke alarm and knows how to disarm it quickly.

This is a deep commitment to continuous self-maintenance. It is the practice of repeatedly choosing the quiet observer over the hysterical voice. It is a choice you make again and again and again.

And that choice, repeated over time, becomes your new baseline.

The maintenance is the peace. The effort is the reward. Keep showing up for the long game. It is the only game that truly matters.

DISCOVERED: THE ULTIMATE REALIZATION THAT PEACE ISN'T ACQUIRED, BUT UNCOVERED (THE POWERFUL SUMMARY)

We have chased peace.

We have hunted it down.

We thought it lived somewhere external.

We believed it was a destination.

We treated it like a major achievement.

That was the central error we made, the $9,000 mistake that cost us everything.

Peace is not acquired.

It is not a prize you earn after years of silent meditation.

It is not a medal pinned to your chest for excellent behavior.

It is uncovered.

Think of it like this: your mind is an old, valuable painting. It is perfect underneath. But over the years, the environment has layered it with grime, smoke, and noise. The paint is still there. The beauty is inherent.

You do not need to paint a new picture.

You need the code to clean the canvas.

What we did in this manual was subtract the noise.

We did not strive to become peaceful.

We strove to remove what blocked the peace.

We identified the malfunctioning smoke alarm.

We defused the thoughts that were not true.

We released the illusion of control.

We recognized the futility of wishing things were different.

Every single tool we used, from the Stoic prompts to the Absurdity Deflator, was an act of subtraction.

When you remove the clutter—when you stop fusing with the screaming committee—what remains?

Peace.

It is the default state.

It is the calm foundation of your awareness.

We started this journey believing we had to fight our way to calm.

We end this journey understanding that calm is what is left when the fight stops.

You are not the storm.

You are the vast, open sky in which the storm appears and disappears.

The tools in this book give you the ability to stand in the sky, observing the weather, without being swept away by the wind.

This is the ultimate realization that sets you free:

You do not need to chase anything anymore.

You do not need to seek a solution that is already installed within you.

The peace is inherent.

It is already yours.

All you have to do is refuse to cover it up with unnecessary noise and worry.

Keep the Code close.

Keep the volume down.

The maintenance continues, but the core work is done.

The peace is uncovered.

GO BE LOUD IN THE WORLD, BUT DO IT WITH A CALM MIND

LOOK AT YOU NOW.

You did the work.

You walked right through the noise.

That was not easy.

We went deep into the messy parts of the brain.

We confronted the smoke alarm.

We stopped pretending that shallow positivity works.

We stopped trying to suppress reality.

You learned how to defuse the thought bomb.

You learned how to take yourself less seriously.

You learned how to breathe when the smoke alarm screams its loudest, most ridiculous shriek.

Remember the promise we made.

You didn't have to become a monk.

You didn't have to trade your fire for fake peace.

You didn't have to delete your honest, brilliant, complex personality.

The world needs that personality.

What you deleted was the unnecessary suffering.

You just found the quiet space inside yourself.

The stable core.

The operational peace.

Go live your life now.

Use that energy we reclaimed from the control illusion.

Go be loud in the world.

Make a glorious mess.

Take the risks you couldn’t take before.

Pursue the passion the fear was hiding.

But do it with a calm mind.

Do it from that stable core.

Keep the code close.

It is always available.

And I’ll be right here if you ever need to come back and turn the page again.

This is continuous maintenance, after all.

Welcome to the quiet.

Now go make some noise.

www.ingramcontent.com/pod-product-compliance
Lightning Source LLC
LaVergne TN
LVHW050914210926
848482LV00012B/437
* 9 7 9 8 2 9 5 5 1 8 4 7 8 *